Best Easy Day Hikes Series

Best Easy Day Hikes
Green Mountains

Eli Burakian

FALCONGUIDES

GUILFORD, CONNECTICUT
HELENA, MONTANA
AN IMPRINT OF GLOBE PEQUOT PRESS

FALCONGUIDES®

Copyright © 2014 Morris Book Publishing, LLC

FalconGuides is an imprint of Globe Pequot Press.
Falcon, FalconGuides, and Outfit Your Mind are registered trademarks of Morris Book Publishing, LLC.

Project editor: Julie Marsh
Layout: Sue Murray
Maps: Melissa Baker © Morris Book Publishing, LLC

Library of Congress Cataloging-in-Publication Data is available on file.

ISBN 978-0-7627-8249-9

Printed in the United States of America
10 9 8 7 6 5 4 3 2 1

Contents

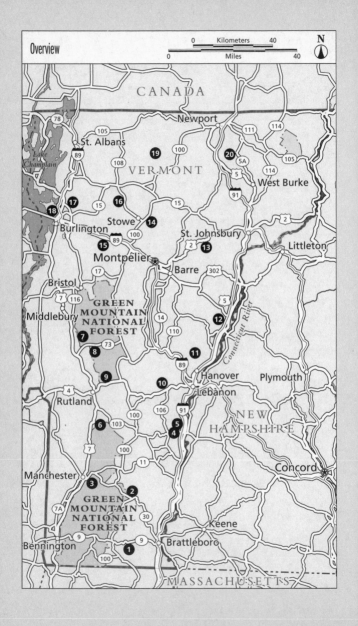

Acknowledgments

I'd like to thank my wife, first and foremost, for putting up with me while I worked on this book during any available hours. Thanks go to my hiking companions, especially Tigran and Otis, who, with their combined eight legs, manage to put in twice the distance on every hike going back and forth and back and forth and . . . I'm also very appreciative of all the hard work that went into creating and maintaining these trails, so I send my dearest thanks to those who helped in any way.

Introduction

The Green Mountains of Vermont are part of the Appalachian Mountain Range, which runs all the way from Georgia up through Maine and into Quebec and Newfoundland. Specifically, the Green Mountains refer to the north-south–running range from northern Massachusetts up through the middle of Vermont. Although there are mountains from a few other ranges and some lone peaks in the state, the term "Green Mountains" generally refers to all the mountains in Vermont, and that is how it is being used in this book.

These Appalachian Mountains used to be much larger, but over hundreds of millions of years, the mountains have been eroded down to the core. Don't let the diminutive elevation of these peaks fool you, though, as the terrain in Vermont can be some of the most challenging in the country. The trails in Vermont tend to be fairly steep, with continuous rocks and roots to be aware of. Luckily, there are also many trails for which the reward is well worth the effort, and the hikes in this book tend to focus on maximizing the reward-to-effort ratio.

This region was inhabited for hundreds of years by Native Americans from the Abenaki culture. Eventually, years of farming and grazing by European settlers and their descendants in Vermont led to a landscape that was more than 80 percent open land by the turn of the twentieth century. As settlers continued moving west and farming became an increasingly small part of the American economy, the Vermont forests grew back, and they now comprise the same percentage of land in the state that grazing land once occupied.

The result of this is hundreds of miles of stone walls crisscrossing the landscape, deep within forests that were once grazing land. Additionally, logging roads of various ages provide paths in the woods, some of which have shifted to those used by hikers and bikers. You will see evidence of this in many of the hikes in this book.

The Green Mountains run north-south through the middle of the state. To the west, much of the state is flanked by Lake Champlain and the Champlain Valley. Farm fields rise dramatically as you progress inland, leading to the steep western slopes of the range. To the east, the Connecticut River Valley creates the border between Vermont and New Hampshire, and in the north on a clear day from the summits in Vermont, the White Mountains of New Hampshire can be seen reaching into the sky. Along the spine of the Greens, five mountains manage to poke their heads above 4,000 feet: Killington Peak, Mt. Abraham, Mt. Ellen, Camel's Hump, and Mt. Mansfield. The summits and ridgelines of the high mountain peaks are often exposed to crazy weather and embody everything that makes Vermont's weather interesting, only more so than in the lower valleys.

In addition to this main range of mountains, other mountains pop up around the state, such as Mt. Equinox, which is part of the Taconic Range, and Mt. Ascutney, which is a monadnock, or lone peak thought to be the remnant of an ancient volcano.

The hiking in Vermont is very varied, ranging from flat walks around lakes to wind-exposed ridgelines to steep trails zigzagging through the forest. A 272-mile long-distance hiking trail, called the Long Trail, traverses the high peaks of the Green Mountains and stretches from the Massachusetts border in the south to the border of Quebec in the north.

The Appalachian Trail, a much longer trail that extends from Georgia to Maine, follows the southern 100 miles of the Long Trail and then turns east just north of Killington for 46 miles into New Hampshire. Many day hikes use these trails as part of a loop. Additionally, many hundreds of trails exist in the state parks, conserved land, and national forests throughout Vermont.

Use this book to begin your adventure, and for ideas to explore. Be willing to use these as jumping-off points, and use other resources available in books, magazines, and online to discover more places to hike, as well as bike, boat, or ski, among many other fun activities. Most important, take your time and enjoy the beauty of Vermont in all its guises.

The Nature of the Green Mountains

The hikes in this book are fairly gentle in nature, but all hikes in Vermont require a careful eye on the weather. The trails are generally well maintained, but be prepared on even the easiest hikes to step over roots, small streams, and rocks. Understanding your environment will not only make for a safer hike, it will make for a more enjoyable one as well.

Weather

As with most mountainous areas, weather can be very changeable and severe. It is important to look at the weather ahead of your hike. Some hikes might be fine in the rain, while others could become a bit dangerous.

Bad weather can come in from any direction, but much of the time the weather patterns flow from the west. When moist air, along with the extra moisture from Lake Champlain, hits the western side of the Green Mountains, the air is forced up in elevation. As the air rises, then so does the relative humidity, and once the air is saturated, precipitation will follow. This is called the orographic effect and explains why mountains often receive much more precipitation than the surrounding lowlands in the form of both rain and snow.

Additionally, high places are often windier, as the air can flow more freely above the surface, picking up speed. Often summits and ridges are exposed, making the wind feel even more severe. Wind chill is nothing to take lightly, and a nice spring day can quickly feel much colder if the wind picks up.

Rain can occur in any month, and snow usually falls between November and April. That being said, leftover winter snow or even fresh snow can be found near the high peaks well into June and as early as October.

Although most people think hiking is strictly a summer-time activity, many of the hikes in this book can be accomplished year-round with proper preparation. The spring is the perfect time to see wildflowers and nature bursting at its seams. Often the temperatures are very comfortable during this time of year. Some trails may be closed during the "mud season" due to the detrimental effects of erosion, so be sure to respect the posted signs.

During the summer, days are long and you can enjoy the outdoors well into the evenings. Getting to high places can be a nice respite from the stifling heat lower down, and hikes near streams, rivers, and lakes can provide refreshing dips.

For many, the most enjoyable time to hike is during the fall foliage season. From mid-September in the north through mid-November in the southern part of Vermont, the fall foliage can be truly breathtaking. Many types of maple, aspen, ash, beech, birch, and oak provide oranges, reds, yellows, browns, and every shade in between. Hiking during foliage season turns walks through the green tunnels in the forests of the summer into kaleidoscopic journeys. The sometimes oppressive heat from the summer is usually gone by this time, providing refreshingly brisk weather, and the summertime crowds will be all but absent.

Even during winter, hiking can be fun. You may need snowshoes, but tramping through a quiet forest covered in a blanket of snow can be very relaxing. Additionally, since the deciduous trees are leafless during this time of year, views through the forest are more plentiful. The days are short and cold, though, so proper preparation is key.

Critters

The Green Mountains abound with abundant wildlife, but as most of the hiking occurs in forested areas, one has to be on the lookout, and lucky to see some types of wildlife.

Many of the rivers and streams have various types of trout, and I'm often amazed by how far up a small stream some of these fish get. A common sight near ponds is the presence of beavers, and although you may not see a beaver, you will surely come across the evenly gnawed nubs of the trees they use for damming the streams.

Deer are common across Vermont, and if you're lucky, you'll see a moose. They're not incredibly common in Vermont, so keep a lookout during the fall when they're in rut and are looking for food before the winter. Be especially careful along roads at night, where moose sometimes come to get the salt from the road.

Creatures such as porcupines, turtles, bobcats, rabbits, turkeys, and bears, to name a few, all inhabit the woods, fields, and waterways of Vermont. If you take your time and walk quietly through the woods, you are much more likely to see these animals. Respect their space and they will respect yours.

Practice Leave No Trace ethics (see more information on page xv), and follow all posted signs regarding the wildlife. Sometimes our seemingly harmless actions have a more profound effect than we can imagine. Very few animals pose a threat to humans in New England, but it is important not to habituate animals such as bears into thinking trash equals food. Also, be aware if you ever find yourself near a mother and a cub or calf not to get between the two. Protective mothers, of many species, are some of the most fearsome creatures around.

During the spring and summer, many trails around Vermont that have views from cliffs are often closed off due to nesting falcons. Respect the signs, and when you see a soaring falcon making loops in the air, you will understand why you did so. There are even bald eagles in Vermont, and crows and gray jays are just a few of the species of birds you will see soaring near the summits.

And of course, there are insects. From the early spring months to late in the fall, insects are an important part of the ecosystem. Early-morning hikers will often be greeted with webs across the trail that have been created during the night, a true initiation. Butterflies and dragonflies are among a host of flying insects that can be beautiful.

Some insects are not so benign, and being prepared for these can make a hike much more pleasant. The first insects that are bothersome tend to be the black flies. They often hover close to the ground and during spring bite in ferocious little swarms. A nice breeze helps, and so does bug spray. Luckily, black flies are pretty much a short-lived spring phenomenon.

Mosquitoes, on the other hand, seem to flourish throughout the summer. They are usually most aggressive in the evening dusk hours and are more prevalent in areas where there is stagnant water. Again, bug spray works well, and a breeze can help keep them away.

Less obvious but more insidious are the ticks, especially the deer ticks. These ticks can carry Lyme disease, which if not treated can lead to problems later in life. The deer ticks that carry the disease can be so small that they are hard to spot unless you are specifically looking for them. And therein lies the key. After every hike do a thorough check on your clothes and body to make sure there are no ticks. If you hike with dogs, you will most likely encounter ticks transported by them.

Luckily, ticks need to be attached for a day or two before they can transmit the disease, so if you're vigilant, you should have no problem staying Lyme disease free. Additionally, protective measures such as long pants can decrease your chance of providing the tick access to your skin. If you do find one attached, use tweezers to make sure the head is also removed.

Plants and the Ecosystem

Much of the time hiking will be spent in the forest. From ancient oaks to brilliant sugar maples, from the long-needled white pine to the spiky high-elevation spruce, and from the quaking of an aspen tree to the blinding white trunk of a paper birch, the forests in the Green Mountains are diverse and rich with history.

Walking through a shaded pine forest and stepping silently across an open forest floor, or crunching your way through trails deep with dried and drying brown, red, and yellow leaves—the experience of being in a forest is not one experience, but a multitude of sights, sounds, and smells. Take the time to learn the names of trees, and what grows where and why, and your hike will become a richer experience.

You will walk through grassy fields and along the banks of cold mountain lakes, across streams and up rocky slabs, and as you do so, the Green Mountains of Vermont will reveal themselves to be complicated yet intimate places. Although the mountains themselves are extremely old, evidence from recent glacial periods is obvious across the landscape if you know where to look.

There are many mountain streams throughout the Green Mountains. Although many originate from springs, it is important to treat or filter all water, as you never know what may be just upstream. Most plants are benign, but know how to identify poison ivy, especially if hiking at a lower elevation during the summer and fall months.

Safety and Preparation

A safe hike is an enjoyable hike. The most important thing to remember is that if you use common sense to prepare for a hike, you most likely will be just fine. Make sure to look at the weather ahead of time. If it's going to be raining, be prepared by bringing not only a rain jacket but also rain pants and a pack cover of some sort, as well as a change of clothes in case you get wet.

If your hike involves elevation gain, be prepared for increasingly colder temperatures the higher you climb. If there's an open summit, it also means that the summit may be exposed to high wind. Wind may be refreshing on a hot summer day, but during much of the year, wind just serves to make you feel that much colder due to the heat-zapping effect of wind chill.

Make sure that everyone in your party is prepared, as one unprepared hiker can ruin a trip for everyone else. Obviously, make sure you have the proper footwear, as nothing ruins a hike more easily than blisters. Make sure you have enough water either by bringing multiple containers on a long hike or by using purification tablets or a water filter if you plan on refilling while out, as the water is not guaranteed to be safe to drink.

Here is a list of items to consider bringing on any hike.

- ❑ Backpack
- ❑ Hiking boots or sneakers
- ❑ Rain and/or wind gear
- ❑ Extra clothing for warmth
- ❑ Sunglasses
- ❑ Hat
- ❑ Water bottle
- ❑ Snacks
- ❑ Map (and possibly a compass and/or GPS)
- ❑ Insect repellent
- ❑ Sunscreen
- ❑ Mobile phone
- ❑ Emergency kit containing fire starter, knife, bandages, antibacterial ointment, personal medications, headlamp, and water purification tablets

Most important, especially if you are alone, make sure to let somebody know where you will be hiking and when you plan on returning. Although many of the hikes in this book are in the forest, there are often areas with good cell reception, so be sure to bring along a cell phone. Additionally, a smart phone can be used in multiple ways, including functioning as a GPS and map.

Be aware during hunting season. Make sure everyone in your party is wearing bright clothing, and put hunter's orange on any dogs. Check with Vermont Fish and Wildlife for specific dates, and be sure to stay on the trail when hiking during hunting season.

Leave No Trace

To leave no trace of your passing is extremely difficult. It is made more so by repeated disregard of these principles. Most people would agree that a primary reason for going on a day hike is to enjoy nature. Unfortunately, we humans adversely impact nature more than any other species, and the true natural places are becoming less numerous. In order to continue to enjoy what nature provides and to allow hikers in the future to enjoy it as well, along with just doing what is decent, it behooves all hikers to make as little impact as possible while traveling through these natural places.

By following the basic principles listed below and using common sense, you can ensure that the places you visit will remain in their current state, however "natural" that may be.

- Pack out all your trash, including biodegradable items like apple cores, which have as great an impact as other trash. When possible, pick up and remove trash that you come across.

- Avoid going off the trail. This keeps the soil damage and erosion from spreading beyond the narrow route. It takes just a few hikers to create a new route, and when this becomes obvious, it turns into a trail. You'll also decrease your chances of getting poison ivy or ticks by remaining on the trail.

- Use outhouses and bathrooms whenever possible. When it is not possible, then make sure you go well away from the trail and water sources and bury waste deep in the soil.

- Don't pick flowers or destroy living wildlife, and don't remove natural objects.

- Don't feed or approach wild animals.

- Be courteous on the trail to allow people moving in the opposite direction or at quicker speeds to pass. If you need to get off the trail to do this, try to stand on rocks or wood so as not to disturb the trailside plant life.

For more information visit LNT.org.

How to Use This Guide

This guide is designed to be simple and easy to use. Each hike has a map and summary information with the trail's vital statistics, including length, difficulty, and approximate hiking time. Directions to the trailhead (including GPS coordinates) are also provided, along with a general description of what you'll see along the hike. A detailed route finder ("Miles and Directions") sets forth mileages between significant landmarks along the trail.

How the Hikes Were Chosen

This guide describes trails that are accessible to every hiker, whether visiting from out of town or a local resident. The hikes are no longer than 6 miles round-trip, and most are considerably shorter. They range in difficulty from flat excursions perfect for a family outing to more challenging treks into some steeper and rockier terrain in the Green Mountains.

I chose these trails for a number of reasons. They are spread across the state, so you should be able to find at least one option that is not too much of a drive from where you are staying. They are all "easy," but there are a few hikes here that involve a bit of steeper maneuvering. These trails and the more challenging sections are so short that they still qualify as easy day hikes.

Also keep in mind that there are many more trails throughout the state, and most likely other short trails near the ones in the book, so use all available resources to scout out other activities and hikes in the area.

Selecting a Hike

As mentioned in the previous section, "easy" is a relative term, so be sure to read the entire trail description, using both distance and elevation, and also take into account weather conditions, your fitness, and your proximity to determine the best hike. This guide uses **easy, moderate,** and **challenging** within this context to describe the difficulty of the trail. Some easy trails may have short steeper sections, and some challenging trails may be short. However, for the most part, the easier trails are shorter and flatter while the challenging trails involve more climbing and longer distances.

Types of Hikes

The hikes in this book fall into three categories:

Loop starts and finishes at the same trailhead, with no (or very little) retracing of your steps.

Lollipop starts and finishes at the same trailhead, with a segment that retraces your steps (the stick on the end of the loop, hence a lollipop) and a loop.

Out-and-back travels to a specific destination, and then retraces your steps back to the trailhead.

Trail Finder

Best Hikes for Waterfalls

Best Hikes with Water Access

Best Hikes for Solitude

Best Hikes for Great Views

Map Legend

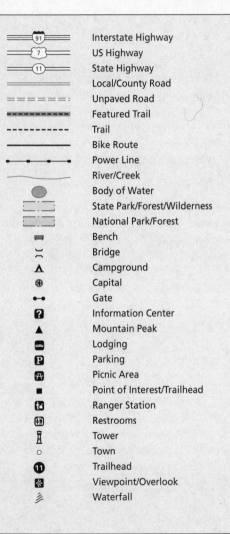	Interstate Highway
	US Highway
	State Highway
	Local/County Road
	Unpaved Road
	Featured Trail
	Trail
	Bike Route
	Power Line
	River/Creek
	Body of Water
	State Park/Forest/Wilderness
	National Park/Forest
	Bench
	Bridge
	Campground
	Capital
	Gate
	Information Center
	Mountain Peak
	Lodging
	Parking
	Picnic Area
	Point of Interest/Trailhead
	Ranger Station
	Restrooms
	Tower
	Town
	Trailhead
	Viewpoint/Overlook
	Waterfall

1   Mt. Olga

With a lookout tower on the top, Mt. Olga has one of the best views in southern Vermont.

Distance: 1.8-mile loop
Hiking time: About 1.5 hours
Elevation gain: 500 feet
Difficulty: Easy
Fees and permits: Day-use fee
Maps: www.vtstateparks.com/pdfs/mollystark_trails.pdf
Trail contact: Vermont State Parks, Molly Stark State Park, (802) 464-5460, www.vtstateparks.com/htm/mollystark.htm; Vermont Department of Forests, Parks and Recreation, Main Office State Parks Division, (802) 522-0841, www.vtfpr.org

Special considerations: The trail leaves from Molly Stark State Park, which is open from mid-May to mid-October. In the winter add another 0.4 mile to the total round-trip, as the closed gate requires a little extra walk. Dogs must be leashed and have proof of rabies vaccination.

Finding the trailhead: The entrance to Molly Stark State Park is on the south side of VT 9, 3.4 miles east of Wilmington and 13.5 miles from exit 2 off I-91 in Brattleboro. Trailhead GPS coordinates: N42 51.162'/W72 48.881'

The Hike

Winter or summer, the view afforded by the fire tower on the summit of Mt. Olga makes this hike well worth the effort. The blue-blazed trail begins across the road from the ranger station. Immediately crossing a small bridge over Beaver Brook, the trail meets up with two stone walls in the first half mile. The trail becomes a little bit steeper until reaching a junction at 0.7 mile.

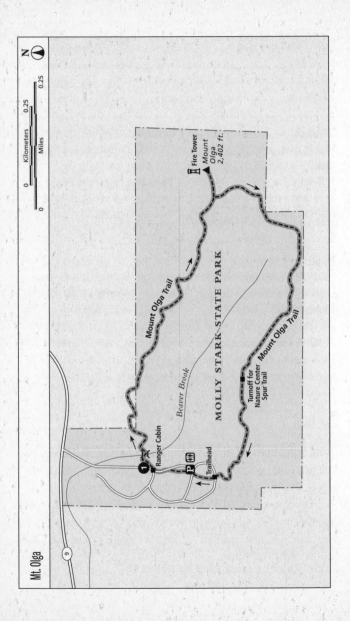

From this junction a short, 0.1-mile spur trail to the summit leads to the base of a tall fire tower. The tower provides incredible views of the mountains in southern Vermont, southern New Hampshire, and northern Massachusetts. Mt. Snow appears close by to the north, and Mt. Monadnock rises high in the east.

One side of Mt. Olga used to be the site of the Hogback Mountain ski area. Although this is no longer functional, a short side trip down an old road from the summit leads a few hundred feet to nice views from the top of the old ski area.

Follow the spur trail back down, and when reaching the junction, this time go straight, passing the trail you came up on the right. The trail gradually descends through a beautiful forest, crossing a small stream and first one and then another turnoff to the Nature Center Spur Trail. Stay on the main trail, and it will pop out of the woods at the south side of the campground and parking area.

Interestingly, although the identity of "Olga" is not known, Molly Stark was the wife of John Stark, an officer in the Revolutionary War. In 1777 during the Battle of Bennington, Molly Stark aided the effort by recruiting men to join her husband and turning her barn into a hospital that helped soldiers on both sides of the conflict.

Miles and Directions

0.0 The Mount Olga Trail starts across from the ranger cabin.

0.7 At the T intersection go left.

0.8 Reach the fire tower at the summit.

0.9 On the return trip, go straight/left at the T intersection.

1.6 Pass a trail junction with a sign saying 0.2 mile to campground.

1.8 Reach the campground and parking lot.

2 West River–Overlook Trail Loop

This loop follows the multiuse West River Trail for a mile along the West River, with informative signs along the way, and passes by some interesting rock formations in the river. The Overlook Trail climbs up over Little Ball Mountain to some scenic views over Jamaica before coming down to an old logging road that goes back to the state park.

Distance: 2.8-mile loop
Hiking time: About 2.5 hours
Elevation gain: 480 feet
Difficulty: Easy to moderate
Fees and permits: Vermont State Parks day-use fee
Maps: USGS Quad: Jamaica
Trail contact: Vermont State Parks, Jamaica State Park, (802) 874-4600, www.vtstateparks .com/htm/ascutney.htm; Vermont Department of Forests, Parks and Recreation, Main Office State Parks Division, (802) 522-0841, www.vtfpr.org
Special considerations: The park is open from early May through Columbus Day. Park outside the gate and follow the road in during the off-season. The West River Trail is a multiuse trail, so be aware of bikers and keep your pets under control.

Finding the trailhead: Take VT 100 to the town of Jamaica. In the center of town, turn north onto Depot Street. After Depot Street crosses the West River, follow the signs into Jamaica State Park. Drive 0.2 mile past the ranger station to the main parking area. Trailhead GPS coordinates: N43 06.562'/W72 46.508'

The Hike

Starting from the end of the parking lot, the West River Trail follows the West River for a few miles along the old bed of the West River Railroad. Just before the trailhead, head down the stairs near the restrooms to check out the Salmon Hole, which is a great swimming hole on a hot summer day.

Interpretive and educational signs dot the West River Trail, along with helpful mileage markers. At 0.6 mile a small viewing deck and a picnic table provide a nice spot to watch kayakers make their way through the "Dumplings," which are large boulders in the middle of the river.

At 1.0 mile from the parking area, the Overlook Trail branches off to the right. The trail climbs steeply for short stretches while passing to the right of a large meadow and to the left of the remains of an old pond.

Near the summit of Little Ball Mountain (1,164 feet) at 1.6 miles, the trail reaches a rock outcrop and steep ledges. Views from these ledges span the West River valley and more of the Green Mountains to the west, while also offering a more intimate perspective on the town of Jamaica. Spur loop trails exist near the summit, but be sure to stay on rocks and these trails, as the vegetation there is easily damaged.

Follow blue blazes as you descend the southern slopes of Little Ball Mountain, reaching a junction near a marshy area at 2.0 miles. Turn right and follow an old logging road back down the mountain, around a fence, and to the Hackberry Lean-to in the campground. The road is just below this lean-to. Take a right and follow it back to the main parking area.

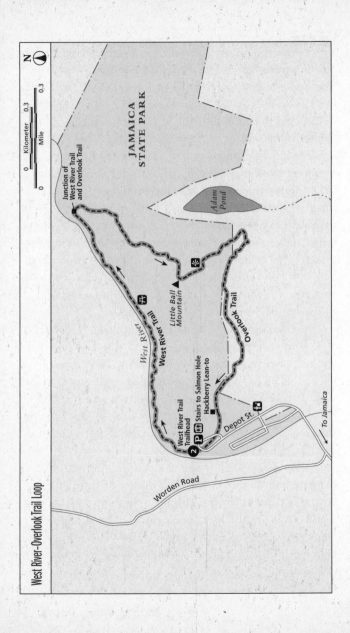

West River-Overlook Trail Loop

JAMAICA STATE PARK

Junction of West River Trail and Overlook Trail

West River

West River Trail

West River Trail

West River Trail Trailhead

Stairs to Salmon Hole
Hackberry Lean-to

Depot St.

Overlook Trail

Little Ball Mountain

Adam Pond

To Jamaica

Worden Road

N

Kilometer   0   0.3

Mile   0   0.3

Miles and Directions

0.0 Start hiking along the West River Trail from the end of the parking area.

0.6 See the large boulders in the river called the "Dumplings" just after passing a nice picnic table above the West River.

1.0 Turn right onto the Overlook Trail.

1.6 Reach a few scenic vistas looking west and south over the town of Jamaica.

2.0 Turn right at a junction onto a logging road.

2.6 The trail ends at the Hackberry Lean-to. Turn right onto the road just below the lean-to.

2.8 Return to where you parked your car.

3 Prospect Rock

This short trail climbs at a steady pace to a rocky outcrop with nice views over Manchester and of Mt. Equinox just to the west.

Distance: 3.2-mile out-and-back
Hiking time: About 2 hours
Elevation gain: About 1,000 feet
Difficulty: Moderate
Fees and permits: None
Maps: USGS Quad: Manchester
Trail contact: Green Mountain National Forest, Rutland Office, (802) 747-6700, www.fs.usda .gov/greenmountain

Special considerations: The trail is actually a very rough road, but the parking for the hike is at the end of the obvious main road across from a house. Follow signs prohibiting parking in the winter, and if necessary, park a little farther down the road.

Finding the trailhead: From the junction of US 7 and VT 11 and 30, follow VT 11 east/30 south 0.4 mile up a hill. Where the road bends left, take a sharp right onto East Manchester Road, and then take an immediate left onto Rootville Road. Follow this road 0.5 mile to a small parking area near a water tower. Trailhead GPS coordinates: N43 10.360'/W73 00.712'

The Hike

Prospect Rock is reached by climbing the old Rootville Road. Follow the obvious road from the parking area to another parking area above. Continue on this road as it gets rougher, and in 0.3 mile you will see a little waterfall off to the right. Above this a short way will be a nice little informal trail that leads to a beautiful set of cascades flowing down angled slabs of rock.

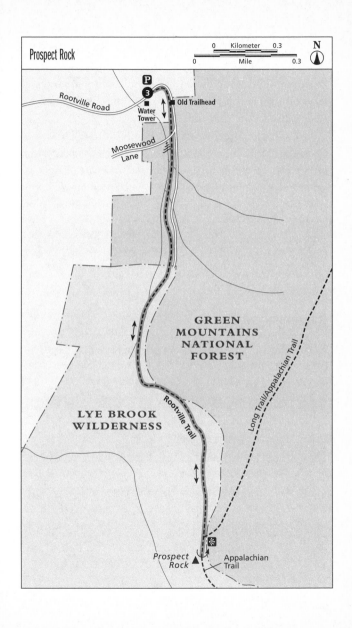

Prospect Rock

0 Kilometer 0.3
0 Mile 0.3

N

Rootville Road

P
3
Water
Tower

Old Trailhead

Moosewood
Lane

GREEN
MOUNTAINS
NATIONAL
FOREST

Rootville Trail

Long Trail/Appalachian Trail

LYE BROOK
WILDERNESS

Prospect
Rock ▲

Appalachian
Trail

Enjoy hiking with your partners, as this is one of the few hikes where the width of the trail allows you to hike side by side. The trail follows along the stream and makes a left turn at around 0.9 mile. Winding up the hill, you will eventually level off on a much more gradual section of road flanked by steep cliffs on the right side.

Follow this road through a beautiful forest. You'll come upon the intersection with the Long Trail on the left, marked by a series of stone steps. Just beyond and to the right is a spur trail out to the viewpoint. If you end up following multiple white blazes, turn around, as you missed the spur.

From here you can see Manchester below and Mt. Equinox high across the valley. Mt. Equinox has a road to the top, and structures are visible. This quick hike provides a nice reward and is close to town. Follow the same route back down to your car.

Miles and Directions

0.0   Leave from the small parking area, and follow the rough road above.

0.1   Pass a kiosk and the upper parking area.

0.3   Reach an informal spur trail to cascades just above a visible lower falls.

0.9   The trail makes a noticeable left turn.

1.6   Reach the junction of the Long Trail and a short spur trail to the right to Prospect Rock.

3.2   Arrive back at your car via the same route.

4 Cascade Falls

The first part of the Weathersfield Trail, which climbs to the peak of Mt. Ascutney, provides a nice short day hike to a large waterfall as well as another small waterfall and a few nice outlooks on the sunny side of the mountain.

Distance: 2.4-mile out-and-back
Hiking time: About 2 hours
Elevation gain: About 700 feet
Difficulty: Easy to the top of the falls (but a very steep, short section if you want to get to the base of the falls)
Fees and permits: None
Maps: USGS Quad: Windsor
Trail contact: Vermont State Parks, Mt. Ascutney State Park, (802) 674-2060,
www.vtstateparks.com/htm/ascutney.htm; Town of West Windsor, (802) 484-7271, www.westwindsorvt.govoffice2.com; Vermont Department of Forests, Parks and Recreation, Main Office State Parks Division, (802) 522-0841, www.vtfpr.org
Special considerations: Do not cross the stream above the waterfall in high water.

Finding the trailhead: From exit 8 on I-91, travel 3.3 miles west on VT 131 to Cascade Falls Road on the right. After a few hundred feet, turn left onto High Meadow Road and follow it 0.3 mile to a turn and parking area on the right. Trailhead GPS coordinates: N43 25.617' / W72 27.985'

The Hike

This hike uses the Weathersfield Trail, which is the only trail that climbs to the top of Mt. Ascutney from the south side of the mountain. It is an easy out-and-back to the top of the falls, but to get to the bottom, you will need to cross over the stream. Do so away from the lip of the falls and only when the water level is low. The descent from the top to the bottom of the falls is very steep.

From the parking lot follow the Weathersfield Trail through a nice open pine forest. The trail reaches a stream with beautiful cascades flowing over slabs of rock. This is the bottom of Little Cascade Falls, which are more just a series of nice rock cascades. Follow the trail over the stream, and soon it will switch back to cross over the stream once again in a rock cleft. Use the provided stairs to reach a beautiful outlook at 0.4 mile.

The Weathersfield Trail is much more gradual from here, contouring around the mountain and only gaining and losing a little bit of elevation over the next half mile or so. At 1.1 miles the Weathersfield Trail heads to the right to continue climbing the mountain. Instead, head to the stream and to the small clearing.

A beautiful vista with long-range views to the south awaits at the top of the waterfall. You can get right up to the lip and sit on a nice boulder enjoying the vista.

To see Cascade Falls from the bottom requires crossing over the stream and following a very steep informal trail along the west side of the falls. At the bottom of the descent, follow another informal trail along the edge of the stream up to the base of the falls. Good hiking poles or at least a nice wooden stick will help make the descent easier.

The falls drop 84 feet over a sheer cliff; they can be very large in the spring but often become a trickle by late summer. Since the whole hike is on the south side of the mountain, this area tends to receive a lot of sun and can be a good early-season hike once the ice is gone.

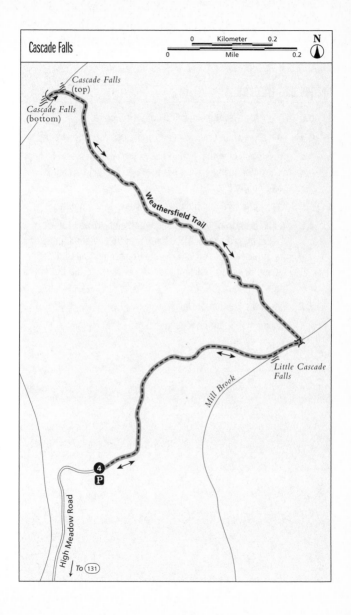

Cascade Falls

Cascade Falls (top)

Cascade Falls (bottom)

Weathersfield Trail

Little Cascade Falls

Mill Brook

4 P

High Meadow Road

To 131

0   Kilometer   0.2

0   Mile   0.2

N

Return the way you came back down to the parking lot, or if you're adventurous, follow the Weathersfield Trail up to the summit to get an even grander view.

Miles and Directions

0.0 Follow the Weathersfield Trail into the woods.

0.3 Reach the Little Cascade Falls and cross over the stream.

0.4 Cross back over the stream above the Little Cascade Falls in a rock cleft using a short set of stairs, reaching a nice viewpoint on the left.

0.6 Reach one of a few outlooks with views to the south.

1.1 Reach the top of the falls. The Weathersfield Trail turns upstream, but to reach the bottom of the waterfall, cross the stream and head down a steep informal trail to a flatter section of water. Follow the stream back up to the bottom of the waterfall.

1.2 Reach the bottom of Cascade Falls.

2.4 Arrive back at the parking lot via the same route.

5   Mt. Ascutney Summit Loop

This short loop from the top of the auto road provides a number of rewards. You will pass by a hang glider launch, a number of viewpoints including an observation tower near the summit, and an interesting walk through a small slot canyon.

Distance: 1.7-mile loop
Hiking time: About 1.5 hours
Elevation gain: About 400 feet
Difficulty: Easy
Fees and permits: Day-use fee to access road to parking lot
Maps: USGS Quad: Windsor
Trail contact: Vermont State Parks, Mt. Ascutney State Park,

(802) 674-2060, www.vtstate parks.com/htm/ascutney.htm; Vermont Department of Forests, Parks and Recreation, Main Office State Parks Division, (802) 522-0841, www.vtfpr.org
Special considerations: The Mt. Ascutney auto road is closed in late fall, winter, and early spring.

Finding the trailhead: Turn off I-91 at exit 8. Head east on VT 131 toward Claremont, NH, but in less than a half mile, turn left, heading north on US 5 for 1.2 miles. Take a left on Back Mountain Road (aka VT 44A) and travel another 1.2 miles to the entrance of Mt. Ascutney State Park on the left. Once in the park, take the Mt. Ascutney auto road up a steep winding route 3.5 miles to the parking lot. Trailhead GPS coordinates: N43 26.387' / W72 27.161'

The Hike

The loop from the top of the Mt. Ascutney auto road is a great way to get big mountain views with small mountain effort. Mt. Ascutney (3,144 feet) is a monadnock because it stands alone and, unlike most mountains in Vermont, is not part of a range. It is thought that Mt. Ascutney may be the core of a very old volcano. The 2,000-acre Mt. Ascutney State Park was developed in the 1930s by the Civilian Conservation Corps.

There are a number of points of interest along the way, making this a great hike for families. Be sure to read the signs carefully, though, as the summit of Mt. Ascutney is a labyrinth of trails.

Head straight up a short incline from the trailhead at the north end of the parking lot. At the first junction head left (west) on the Hang Glider Trail. When this meets the Weathersfield Trail, head straight onto two short spurs leading to amazing views from the West Peak and the hang glider launch. In the summer you may be lucky enough to watch people launch their hang gliders off a seemingly vertical cliff above the forest. Due to the road access, Mt. Ascutney is a major launch site for many hang-gliding pilots.

Returning from the viewpoint on the spur trail, go left (east) at the junction, following the Weathersfield Trail 0.3 mile up a decent climb to an intersection near the summit at 0.9 mile. To the right is the summit, covered by numerous radio and television towers. To the left is the observation tower.

From the observation tower there are expansive views to Okemo in the west, Killington in the north, the Connecticut River valley and much of New Hampshire to the east, and Stratton and the rest of southern Vermont to the south.

Continue following signs to the Slot Trail, passing by a junction to the Slab Trail on the right and a short spur trail to Brownsville Rock on the left. You will pass by some big moss-covered rocks. At the next intersection at 1.3 miles, take a sharp right and follow the Slot Trail back toward the parking lot. You will pass through a slot between two

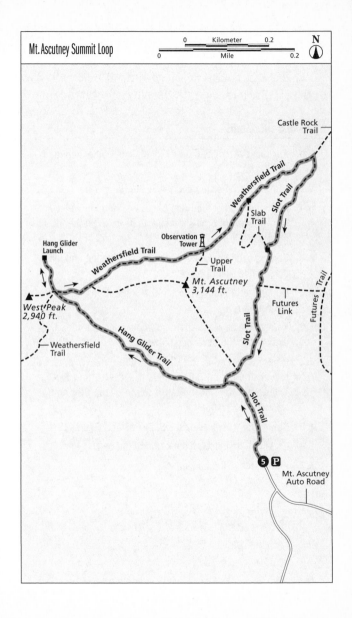

Mt. Ascutney Summit Loop

Kilometer

Mile

N

Castle Rock
Trail

Weathersfield Trail

Slot Trail

Slab
Trail

Hang Glider
Launch

Observation
Tower

Weathersfield Trail

Upper
Trail

Mt. Ascutney
3,144 ft.

Futures Trail

West Peak
2,940 ft.

Futures
Link

Weathersfield
Trail

Hang Glider Trail

Slot Trail

Slot Trail

5 P

Mt. Ascutney
Auto Road

rocks, which provides the name to the trail. Continue going straight, passing by signs for the Slab Trail and the Futures Link.

At the final intersection turn left and head back down to the parking lot.

Miles and Directions

0.0 Begin at the trailhead on the north side of the auto road parking lot.

0.1 Turn left at a junction and follow the Hang Glider Trail.

0.4 At the junction of the Hang Glider Trail and the Weathersfield Trail, go straight on a short spur to a view from the hang glider launch.

0.6 Coming back from hang glider launch, turn left and follow the Weathersfield Trail.

0.9 Go right at a junction to tag the summit and see the radio towers.

1.0 Back at the same junction, now go straight for a few hundred feet to the observation tower.

1.3 Continue following the trail from the observation tower toward the Brownsville, Windsor, Futures, and Slot Trails. Turn right at the intersection of the Slot and Castle Rock Trails.

1.5 Stay straight, bypassing the Slab Trail and Futures Link.

1.6 Go left at the junction, back toward the parking lot.

1.7 Arrive back at the parking lot.

6 White Rocks Ice Beds Trail

This trail really packs a punch. First, there's a short climb to incredible views of a huge rock slide and the giant White Rocks Cliff, and then it's down to the bottom of the rock slide, where snow and ice get trapped and can often be found into summer, providing nature's air conditioner.

Distance: 1.8-mile out-and-back
Hiking time: About 1.5 hours
Elevation gain: 450 feet
Difficulty: Easy to moderate
Fees and permits: None
Maps: USGS Quad: Wallingford
Trail contact: Green Mountain National Forest, Rutland Office, (802) 747-6700, www.fs.usda .gov/greenmountain; USDA Forest Service National Recreation Areas, www.fs.usda .gov/recarea/greenmountain/ null/recarea/?recid=64989 &actid=50

Special considerations: The picnic area gate, which provides access to the trailhead, is open from 6 a.m. to 10 p.m.

Finding the trailhead: Take VT 140 to Sugar Hill Road, 2.1 miles east of US 7 in Wallingford and 4 miles west of VT 103 in East Wallingford. If you're coming from the east, the turn will be a sharp left; from the west it is a slight right. Follow Sugar Hill Road for about 200 feet, and then turn right on a road that has signs for Green Mountain National Forest White Rocks Picnic Area. Trailhead GPS coordinates: N43 27.051' / W72 56.618'

The Hike

On this great multifaceted hike, there's something for everyone. Kids are sure to love "nature's air conditioner," and multiple viewpoints along the way keep everyone interested. A picnic area at the trailhead is the perfect place for a post-hike

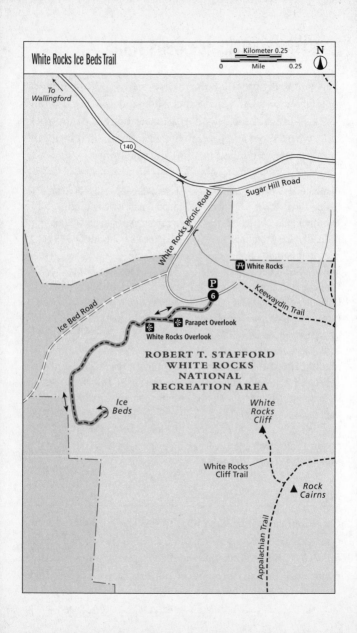

White Rocks Ice Beds Trail

0   Kilometer 0.25

0   Mile   0.25

N

To
Wallingford

140

Sugar Hill Road

White Rocks Picnic Road

White Rocks

P
6

Keewaydin Trail

Ice Bed Road

Parapet Overlook

White Rocks Overlook

ROBERT T. STAFFORD
WHITE ROCKS
NATIONAL
RECREATION AREA

Ice
Beds

White
Rocks
Cliff

White Rocks
Cliff Trail

Rock
Cairns

Appalachian Trail

meal. Note that this was recently named the Robert T. Stafford White Rocks National Recreation Area after the late Vermont governor and senator.

The trail leaves from the back corner of the parking lot. After quickly crossing over a small stream, the trail makes several switchbacks up to a knoll. At 0.2 mile a very short spur trail leads to the Parapet Overlook, which has amazing views of the rock slides about which this national recreation area is named. At the top of a knoll, go straight ahead as the trail turns right to another amazing view from White Rocks Overlook.

Head down the other side of the rise while following the trail through a spruce forest. The trail bends to the left and meets up with an old woods road. Follow this down to a small bridge over a stream, and then head back up the stream on the other side to the base of the rock slide. Snow can often be found here late into summer, and the cool air and water flow down the ravine all summer.

Enjoy the air conditioning, play on the rocks at the slide if you are so inclined, and then head back up the way you came.

Miles and Directions

0.0   The trail leaves from the back of the parking lot.

0.2   A spur trail leads 50 yards to views from the Parapet Overlook.

0.3   Reach the White Rocks Overlook, with a slightly different view of the cliffs.

0.6   Meet up with an old woods road.

0.8   After crossing the stream, turn left and follow the other side.

0.9   Reach the bottom of the rock slide.

1.8   Arrive back at the parking lot via the same route.

7 Falls of Lana and Rattlesnake Cliffs

This hike takes you to the incredible Falls of Lana, which deserve exploring, and possibly even to a pool for swimming below the main falls. Additionally, you'll visit the beautiful Rattlesnake Cliffs viewpoint, where a high perch above Lake Dunmore provides incredible views over Silver Lake, as well as the Vermont Valley and the Adirondacks in New York.

Distance: 4.5-mile lollipop
Hiking time: About 2.5 to 4 hours (depending on whether you explore the falls)
Elevation gain: About 1,200 feet
Difficulty: Moderate to difficult
Fees and permits: None
Maps: USGS Quad: East Middlebury
Trail contact: Green Mountain National Forest, Rutland Office, (802) 747-6700, www.fs.usda.gov/greenmountain
Special considerations: The cliffs are closed during peregrine falcon nesting season from March 15 through August 1. During this time it is still worth exploring the waterfalls. It is also worth exploring the surrounding area including Silver Lake, which is a great place to camp.

Finding the trailhead: From Middlebury travel 6.7 miles south on US 7 to VT 53 south. Go left onto VT 53 and drive 3.8 miles south, and the parking lot is on the left just past Branbury State Park. From Rutland take U.S. 7 north to Brandon and turn right onto VT 73. Take this for 3 miles and turn left on VT 53 north. If you're traveling from the east, travel on VT 73 for 14 miles from VT 100, and then turn right on VT 53 north. On VT 53 north the parking area will be on the right in 5.25 miles. If you see Branbury State Park, you've gone too far. Trailhead GPS coordinates: N43 54.028' / W73 03.853'

The Hike

With incredible views from a beautiful cliff-top perch to swimming in a pool below a big waterfall, this hike has it all. If you are here during peregrine falcon nesting, the trip to the waterfall is still well worth it even if you cannot get to the cliff.

Note: Heading down to the falls on either side will increase the total distance, but it is well worth the excursion.

Leaving from the parking lot, you'll head through the woods to a gravel trail, passing a sign for the Silver Lake Recreation Area and the Falls of Lana and reaching a clearing for power lines and a big water pipe with views of Lake Dunmore at 0.3 mile. Just past this you'll see trails down to the left. Following these down to an obvious overlook, you'll get a good view of the Falls of Lana dropping down into a big pool. You can continue to follow trails down this side to get to the pool, which can be an exciting place for a dip. Following the increasingly steep trails farther down the side, you can work your way to the bottom of the falls, where you see Sucker Brook pouring through a little slot as it turns right below the swimming hole.

From the junction of the spur trail, continue on the main trail to Rattlesnake Cliffs, following the stream and passing by some pleasant pools, past the junction with the Silver Lake Trail to a bridge at 0.6 mile. Across the bridge turn right, where you will see another spur trail down to the left that heads to the other side of the falls. To get to the cliffs, head right from the bridge, soon passing the Aunt Jennie Trail junction on the left. At the junction with the North Branch Trail in a field at 0.9 mile, turn left, continuing on the Rattlesnake Cliffs Trail.

You'll follow a ravine up along a stream, crossing it soon after the junction and again three quarters of a mile later after climbing through the woods. The trail turns southwest after crossing the stream and contours along the side of the mountain until reaching the upper junction of the Aunt Jennie Trail at 2.0 miles. After a short switchback you'll reach the junction with the Oak Ridge Trail, which leads to the summit of Mt. Moosalamoo. Pass this, and soon you'll reach a sign with a spur to the left heading to Rattlesnake Point.

Make a big switchback down to the cliffs and enjoy the magnificent view over Lake Dunmore. Silver Lake seemingly floats above the beautiful valley. To the west the Adirondacks form a wall of mountains, with the Taconics visible to their south. From here you can follow the cliff for a precarious scramble up to Sid's Point, or you can retrace your steps and turn left at the junction for a short trip out to another great view.

Follow the trail back the way you came, and in less than a half mile, turn right onto the Aunt Jennie Trail, which is a slightly steeper route back around. In just under a mile, you'll hit the Rattlesnake Cliffs Trail. Turn right and follow this down over the bridge, past the falls, and to the parking lot.

Miles and Directions

0.0 Leave from the north end of the parking lot and follow a trail into the woods, turning right onto a gravel path.

0.3 Reach a clearing crossed by a water pipe and power lines.

0.4 Reach the Falls of Lana overlook spur. Head down through the woods to check out the waterfalls. The farther you go down, the more you will see.

0.5 Stay straight on the Rattlesnake Cliffs Trail at the junction of the Silver Lake Trail.

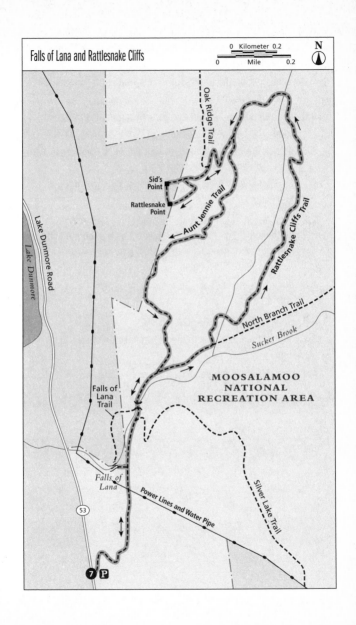

Falls of Lana and Rattlesnake Cliffs

0   Kilometer   0.2

0   Mile   0.2

N

Oak Ridge Trail

Sid's Point

Rattlesnake Point

Aunt Jennie Trail

Rattlesnake Cliffs Trail

North Branch Trail

Sucker Brook

Lake Dunmore

Lake Dunmore Road

MOOSALAMOO
NATIONAL
RECREATION AREA

Falls of
Lana Trail

Falls of
Lana

Power Lines and Water Pipe

Silver Lake Trail

53

7 P

0.6 Reach a footbridge over Sucker Brook. Cross over the bridge and take a right. (A spur trail from here leads to the other side of the Falls of Lana.)

0.7 Stay right on the Rattlesnake Cliffs Trail at the junction with the Aunt Jennie Trail.

0.9 In the middle of a field at a turnoff with the North Branch Trail, head left, following the sign to Rattlesnake Cliffs.

2.0 Reach the upper intersection with the Aunt Jennie Trail. Continue straight to Rattlesnake Cliffs.

2.2 At the intersection with the Oak Ridge Trail, turn left to the cliffs.

2.3 Turn left at an intersection, following a switchback out to Rattlesnake Point. Follow the precarious trail up the cliff to Sid's Point or head back to the last junction and turn left for a short trip to Sid's Point.

2.5 Return to the outlook junction and head back down the same trail.

2.9 Turn right onto the Aunt Jennie Trail.

3.8 Reach the junction with the Rattlesnake Cliffs Trail. Turn right.

4.5 Arrive back at the parking lot.

8 Mt. Horrid's Great Cliff

This short and fairly steep trail follows the Long Trail to the Great Cliff, which affords views east into New Hampshire and west into New York.

Distance: 1.4-mile out-and-back
Hiking time: About 1.5 hours
Elevation gain: 640 feet
Difficulty: Moderate
Fees and permits: None
Maps: USGS Quad: Mount Carmel
Trail contact: Green Mountain Club, (802) 244-7037, www.greenmountainclub.org; Green Mountain National Forest, Rutland Office, (802) 747-6700, www.fs.usda.gov/greenmountain
Special considerations: Peregrine falcons may be nesting near the cliff, and the trail is usually closed from March 15 through August 1. Please observe all posted signs so as not to disturb the birds. Keep control of any dogs, as you'll need to cross over a busy road.

Finding the trailhead: From VT 100 in Rochester, head west on VT 73 for 9.3 miles. If you're coming from US 7 in the west, head east for 8.2 miles on VT 73. The parking area is located on the south side of VT 73 where it crests over Brandon Gap. The trail begins across the road on the north side. Trailhead GPS coordinates: N43 50.383' / W72 58.119'

The Hike

This hike up a short but fairly steep section of the Long Trail takes hikers to incredible views, with Mt. Moosilauke and the White Mountains visible to the east and the Adirondacks in New York equally as lofty to the west.

Below the cliff the road is visible winding down the mountain, while a marsh and pond below may provide opportunities to see wildlife.

From the parking lot on the south side of VT 73, safely cross the road to a short trail leading to a posted sign for the Long Trail. Follow this east for a little bit, and then head north through the woods, coming to the trail register at 0.1 mile. As peregrine falcons like to nest in high places and Vermont has been working hard to protect the once decimated population, the cliff will most likely be closed between March 15 and August 1, and signs will be posted here. Please respect all posted signs.

The trail continues up fairly steeply past a sign at 0.2 mile noting your entrance into the Joseph Battell Wilderness. You'll wind through a beautiful birch and maple forest. This trail makes for a great outing during fall foliage season.

After briefly mellowing out for a short while, at 0.5 mile the trail comes to the steepest section, where stone steps lead upward. At 0.6 mile the blue-blazed spur trail to the cliffs branches off to the right. Follow that up a short, steep section, and soon you'll arrive at the breathtaking cliff-top view. On a clear day you can see Mt. Moosilauke to the east rising up from the Connecticut River valley, while to the west the southern end of Lake Champlain divides Vermont and the Adirondack Mountains.

Follow the trail back down the same way. Be careful crossing the road as cars come by quickly.

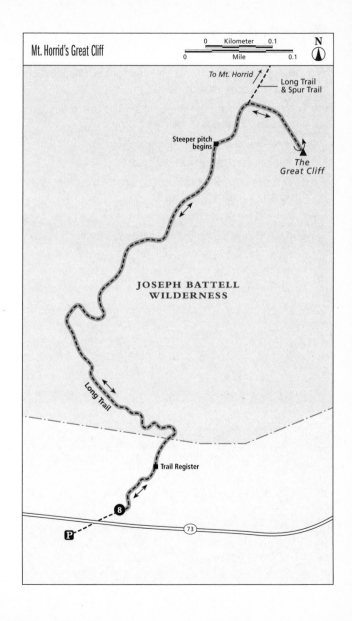

Mt. Horrid's Great Cliff

Kilometer

0   0.1

Mile

0   0.1

N

To Mt. Horrid

Long Trail
& Spur Trail

The
Great Cliff

Steeper pitch
begins

JOSEPH BATTELL
WILDERNESS

Long Trail

Trail Register

8

P

73

Miles and Directions

0.0 Cross the road from the parking lot to get to the official trail-head of the Long Trail; then head east and quickly turn north into the woods following the trail.

0.1 Reach the trail register, where signs will be posted if the cliffs are closed due to peregrine falcon nesting.

0.2 Enter the Joseph Battell Wilderness.

0.5 Begin a steep section with stone steps.

0.6 At a sign to the Great Cliff, turn right on the blue-blazed trail as the Long Trail continues left.

0.7 Arrive at the Great Cliff.

1.4 Arrive back at the parking lot via the same route.

9 Deer Leap Rock

Deer Leap Rock provides an amazing view above Sherburne Pass across to Pico Mountain. The 1.1 miles to the overlook ends just a few hundred yards above the trailhead, but the reward is well worth the small effort to get there. Finish the hike with beer or a meal at the Inn at Long Trail, a favorite spot for locals for many years.

Distance: 2.2-mile out-and-back
Hiking time: About 1.5 hours
Elevation gain: About 550 feet
Difficulty: Moderate
Fees and permits: None
Maps: USGS Quad: Pico Peak
Trail contact: Green Mountain Club, (802) 244-7037,
www.greenmountainclub.org; Green Mountain National Forest, Rutland Office, (802) 747-6700, www.fs.usda.gov/greenmountain
Special considerations: The trail leaves from US 4, a busy road, so if you have pets, keep them leashed until farther into the trail.

Finding the trailhead: The trail leaves from the top of Sherburne Pass on US 4, 31 miles west of I-89 exit 1 and 9 miles east of the intersection of US 7 in Rutland. Parking is located next to the Inn at Long Trail on the north side of US 4; if the spaces provided for hikers are full, park in the lot on the south side of the road. The trailhead is located on the right (east) side of the inn. Trailhead GPS coordinates: N43 39.843'/W72 49.939'

The Hike

The beginning part of this hike used to be part of the Appalachian and Long Trails until this section was relocated a few years ago. With a somewhat rocky beginning, the

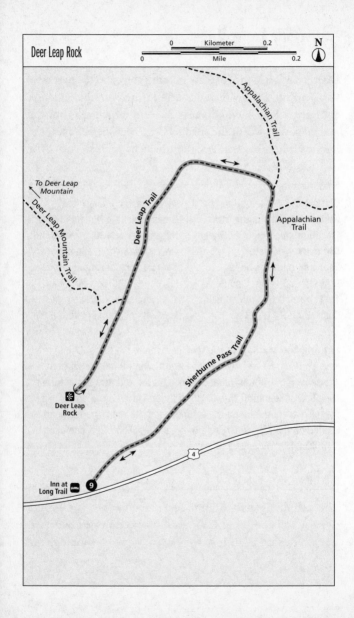

Deer Leap Rock

0 Kilometer 0.2
0 Mile 0.2

N

To Deer Leap
Mountain

Deer Leap Mountain Trail

Deer Leap Trail

Appalachian
Trail

Appalachian
Trail

Sherburne Pass Trail

Deer Leap
Rock

4

Inn at
Long Trail

9

blue-blazed trail climbs northeast, briefly paralleling US 4, and then ascends away from the road to head north. It veers back to the south to end at an amazing overlook, with Pico Mountain rising dramatically across the road.

The trail leaves just behind and to the right of the Inn at Long Trail. The very beginning is rocky, but it shortly mellows out. Ascend the slope for a half mile until you reach two junctions in quick succession. (You will be on the Appalachian Trail for a few hundred feet.) Turn left at both junctions and follow the Deer Leap Trail out toward the overlook. At 0.9 mile you will reach another junction. Stay left/straight and follow the trail 0.2 mile to the overlook.

Deer Leap Rock overlook is a great place to have a picnic on a sunny day. The rock shines brightly as the quartz in the granite reflects the light, making the rock almost appear to glow to observers from below and across the road.

Return by the same route and enjoy a beer and/or meal at the Inn at Long Trail, a locals' favorite.

Miles and Directions

0.0 Start at the Sherburne Pass trailhead next to the Inn at Long Trail.

0.5 Go left at the junction with the Appalachian Trail and old Long Trail, and then left again onto the Deer Leap Trail.

0.9 Stay straight at the junction, following a sign that says 0.2 mile to the overlook.

1.1 Reach Deer Leap Rock overlook.

2.2 Arrive back at the trailhead via the same route.

10 Mt. Tom Loop

This hike provides a number of nice views to the south, east, and west while climbing the Faulkner Trail to the South Peak of Mt. Tom. The route wraps around the North Peak through the woods in Billings Park and meets up with the Faulkner Trail again.

Distance: 3.2-mile lollipop
Hiking time: About 2.5 hours
Elevation gain: About 800 feet
Difficulty: Moderate
Fees and permits: None
Maps: USGS Quad: Woodstock South & Woodstock North
Trail contact: Marsh-Billings-Rockefeller National Historical Park, (802) 457-3368, www.nps.gov/mabi/index.htm;

Town of Woodstock, (888) 496-1601, www.woodstockvt.com
Special considerations: The Faulkner Trail is very graded, but do not shortcut the switchbacks, as it erodes the trail. Also, there are a lot of trails in this area, so bring a compass, GPS, or smart phone to keep track of where you are.

Finding the trailhead: Take US 4 to Woodstock. If you are coming from the east, at the green in the center of town, turn right onto Mountain Avenue and drive 0.4 mile to Faulkner Park. If you're coming from the west, circle around the green to get on Mountain Avenue. Trailhead GPS coordinates: N43 37.401'/W72 31.555'

The Hike

This relatively easy hike up and around Mt. Tom in the heart of Woodstock begins on the Faulkner Trail, which leaves from Faulkner Park. The first half of the trip is a very graded ascent, with the second half a more traditional meander through the woods.

Follow the Faulkner Trail straight back out of the park, and climb the many switchbacks up the hill. It makes its way up the side of the mountain at a very leisurely pace. Pass by a number of adjoining trails, and take a break on one of the many benches. At 1.4 miles there is a nice place to stop and catch some views.

At this point the trail starts to climb a bit more steeply, and at one point near the top, a steel cable aids hikers on a particularly steep and rocky section. This is the only slightly technical part of the hike, so know that once you're on top, the rest is easier than what you just did.

At the top of the South Peak (1.6 miles), you'll see a big electric star. Turn left onto the Mt. Tom Road. From here you get a fantastic view to the west. Follow this road north as it gently slopes down. At 1.8 miles turn right at a sign that reads To BILLINGS TRAIL. Take this trail, and stay right as you follow signs for the Billings Trail.

The Billings Trail wraps around the north summit of Mt. Tom, making a 180-degree turn. At 2.1 miles turn right at a junction with the North Peak Trail, continuing to follow signs for the Billings Trail. Take your time here, as the trail descends rather quickly. At 2.4 miles turn left on the Precipice Trail, and very shortly thereafter turn right onto the Upper Link Trail.

Continue to follow this trail until you see a sign on the left to the Lower Link Trail. This leads back to the Faulkner Trail at 2.7 miles. Take the Faulkner Trail back to the trailhead at Faulkner Park.

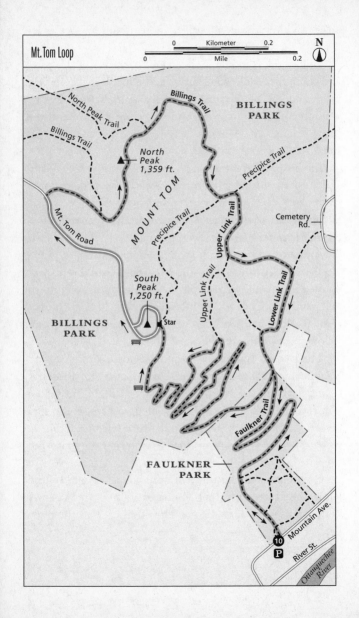

0   Kilometer   0.2

0   Mile   0.2

N

North Peak Trail

Billings Trail

BILLINGS PARK

Billings Trail

North Peak 1,359 ft.

MOUNT TOM

Precipice Trail

Precipice Trail

Mt. Tom Road

Upper Link Trail

Upper Link Trail

Cemetery Rd.

Lower Link Trail

South Peak 1,250 ft.

Star

BILLINGS PARK

Faulkner Trail

FAULKNER PARK

Mountain Ave.

10

P

River St.

Ottauquechee River

Miles and Directions

0.0 The trail leaves from Faulkner Park in Woodstock.

0.5 At the junction of the Lower Link Trail, stay left on the Faulkner Trail.

1.2 At the junction of the Upper Link Trail, stay left on the Faulkner Trail.

1.4 Reach a bench with views to the south and east.

1.6 Reach the South Peak of Mt. Tom and the star installation. Go left on Mt. Tom Road.

1.8 Turn right at a small trail with a sign reading To BILLINGS TRAIL.

2.1 At the junction with the North Peak Trail, stay right on the Billings Trail.

2.4 Turn left at the junction with the Precipice Trail.

2.5 Go straight/right, following a sign for the Upper Link Trail.

2.6 Go left at a junction, continuing on the Lower Link Trail.

2.7 Meet back up with the Faulkner Trail.

3.2 Arrive back at Faulkner Park.

11 Gile Mountain

The hike up Gile Mountain is a great short hike for families. With no steep sections and an observation tower on the summit, it rewards hikers of all ages with views of the Connecticut River valley and both New Hampshire and Vermont.

Distance: 1.4-mile out-and-back
Hiking time: About 1 hour
Elevation gain: About 400 feet
Difficulty: Easy
Fees and permits: None
Maps: USGS Quad: South Strafford
Trail contact: Norwich Town Forest through the Town of Norwich, (802) 649-1419, www.norwich.vt.us
Special considerations: Access is via a dirt road, so be prepared in the spring when the road may be muddy. Gile Mountain also has mountain bike trails that occasionally cross the hiking trail, so be aware of bikers.

Finding the trailhead: From exit 13 off I-91, head northwest into the town of Norwich. In 1.25 miles turn left on Turnpike Road. Take Turnpike Road for 5.2 miles. Note that the road turns to dirt after 2.5 miles. The signed parking area is on the left just before a farmhouse on the right. Trailhead GPS coordinates: N43 47.364' / W72 20.568'

The Hike

The trail up to the Gile Mountain fire tower is short and easy, making for a nice rewarding hike for families and children of all ages. The climb begins at a kiosk next to the parking area. Follow the obvious blue-blazed trail through the woods, quickly crossing over a small bridge.

Gile Mountain

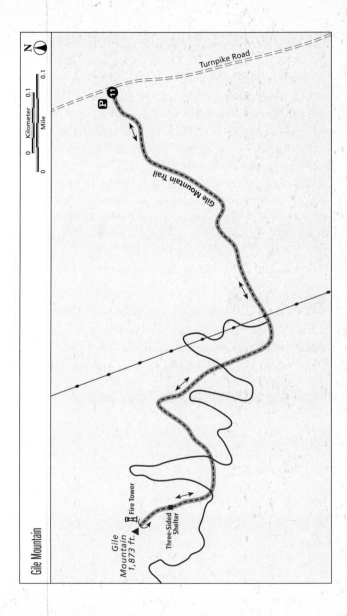

At 0.3 mile the trail crosses a mountain bike trail and then immediately pops out into a large clearing for power lines. You can see nice views of the Connecticut River valley and the surrounding hills in New Hampshire from here.

The trail continues up, making a few switchbacks, and eventually reaches a three-sided wooden shelter. In recent years the cabin has been decorated with graffiti and paintings, some of which are pretty cool. The cabin even has a sign proclaiming it the "Shredd Shack."

Just beyond the cabin is a tall observation tower. From the top of the observation tower, Mt. Ascutney can be seen rising up from the south, while Mt. Moosilauke in New Hampshire is visible to the northeast. On clear days the spine of the Green Mountains in Vermont is visible to the west.

Return the same way back down to the parking lot.

Miles and Directions

0.0 The trail begins at the back of the parking area.

0.3 Pass through an open area with power lines.

0.7 Reach a cabin and then the fire tower a few hundred feet beyond.

1.4 Arrive back at the parking lot via the same route.

12 Bald Top Mountain

This short western approach to a nice summit meadow with eastern views to the White Mountains is part of the 36-mile Cross Rivendell Trail.

Distance: 3.6-mile out-and-back
Hiking time: About 3 hours
Elevation gain: 1,250 feet
Difficulty: Easy to moderate
Fees and permits: None
Maps: USGS Quad: Fairlee

Trail contact: Rivendell Trails Association, (603) 353-2170, www.crossrivendelltrail.org/
Special considerations: This trail is partly shared with a snowmobile trail, so be observant in winter. The roadside pull-off is small, so park considerately.

Finding the trailhead: Take exit 15 on I-91 to Fairlee. Turn right off the interstate if northbound, left if southbound, reaching US 5 in a few hundred feet. Turn right and follow US 5 south for 2.5 miles. Turn right (west) on VT 244 and follow this for 2.6 miles, turning right (north) onto Bloodbrook Road. The trailhead is on the right in 1.6 miles, next to a fence and gate. Trailhead GPS coordinates: N43 55.474'/W72 12.407'

The Hike

Next to the pull-off, head through a gap in the fence and follow the obvious snowmobile trail. Soon a kiosk informs you that, yes, you are on the correct trail, which is the Cross Rivendell Trail. Follow it for a half mile until you reach a sign and a blue blaze informing you that the trail heads left 1.2 miles to the summit.

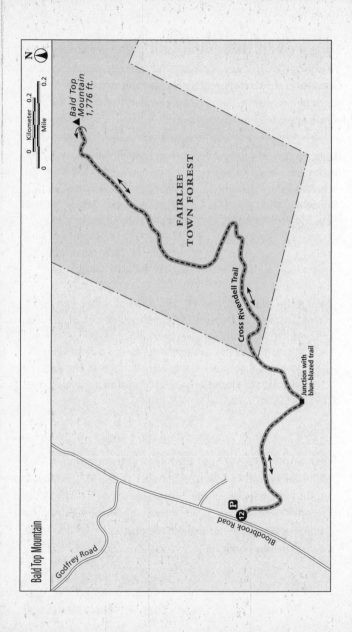

Bald Top Mountain

N

Godfrey Road

Bloodbrook Road

12

P

Junction with
blue-blazed trail

Cross Rivendell Trail

FAIRLEE
TOWN FOREST

▲ Bald Top
Mountain
1,776 ft.

0   Kilometer   0.2

0   Mile   0.2

Take this trail for another 0.2 mile, and then be sure to take the path on the right that diverges from the small woods road. After a climb and a few switchbacks, the trail heads into a ravine that climbs into a beautiful hardwood forest with large old-growth trees.

Just beyond this the trail climbs up a short stair and then follows the contour of the mountain, eventually emerging from the forest onto a snowmobile trail. This wraps up and around, leading to the open summit. Although there is not much of a view to the west, there are nice views to the east of the mountains above the Connecticut River, Smarts Mountain, and Mt. Cube, as well as the westernmost above-tree-line summit in the White Mountains, Mt. Moosilauke.

Follow the same route back down. Take care that you are on the correct trail, as a number of trails join at the summit. (*Option:* Continuing on the Cross Rivendell Trail east down the other side of the mountain leads 3.3 miles to the edge of Lake Morey. This could be a feasible car shuttle if you don't want to go back the same way.)

Miles and Directions

0.0   Follow the obvious snowmobile path from the edge of the road.

0.1   Reach a kiosk with information about the trail.

0.5   Go left at the sign onto a blue-blazed trail.

0.7   Stay right on a smaller path.

1.7   Head right onto a snowmobile trail and follow it up to the summit.

1.8   Reach the summit of Bald Top Mountain.

3.6   Arrive back at the trailhead via the same route.

13 Osmore Pond and Big Deer Mountain

This nice, fairly flat loop hike takes you to the summit of Big Deer Mountain, which has fine views of Lake Groton and other mountains to the north, east, and south, and then along Osmore Pond, a beautiful small lake with shelters near the edge.

Distance: 4.3-mile loop

Hiking time: About 2.5 hours

Elevation gain: About 600 feet

Difficulty: Easy

Fees and permits: Vermont State Parks day-use fee

Maps: USGS Quad: Marshfield

Trail contact: Vermont State Parks, New Discovery State Park, (802) 426-3042, www.vtstateparks.com/htm/newdiscovery.htm; Vermont

Department of Forests, Parks and Recreation, Main Office State Parks Division, (802) 522-0841, www.vtfpr.org

Special considerations: As this hike begins and ends in a campground, respect campers' privacy when traveling through and keep pets under control.

Finding the trailhead: The trail leaves from the New Discovery Campground in Groton State Forest. From I-89 take exit 8 then turn right reaching US 2 in 1 mile. Head straight and follow US 2 east for 18 miles to VT 232 on the right just past Marshfield. From I-91 in the north, take exit 21 and follow US 2 west to VT 232. The campground is located 4.4 miles south on VT 232. From I-91 in the south, take exit 17; then follow US 302 west for 8.6 miles and turn right on VT 232. The campground is on the right in 9.1 miles. Once in the campground, find a parking spot after bearing left at site 40. If the gate is open, you can drive another 0.3 mile to the trailhead of the Big Deer Mountain Trail. Trailhead GPS coordinates: N44 19.181'/W72 17.246'

The Hike

At 25,000 acres, the Groton State Forest is the second-largest block of land owned by the state. There are endless trails and many lakes here, so if you visit to hike this loop, you may find other options in the area to keep you busy. The size of this area makes it feel very remote, providing a wilder experience than the 4.3-mile hike may suggest. That being said, this relatively flat loop provides mountain and lakeside views in a hike that is appropriate for anyone.

After you enter New Discovery Campground, the ranger at the gate (during the open season) will let you know where to park and can give you local maps. Assuming you park near site 40, head to the left, following the dirt road toward Peacham Pond. At 0.3 mile turn right into the woods at a sign for Big Deer Mountain.

You'll follow this trail, first downhill and then slightly uphill, past a ruined Civilian Conservation Corps–era shelter to a junction at 1.4 miles. From here head straight as the trail climbs for close to a half mile to the summit of Big Deer Mountain. From the viewpoint at the end of the trail, you can see Lake Groton stretched out in front of you, with sweeping views to the south. Slightly back along the trail, another short spur leads to views to the north and east, including nearby Peacham Pond.

Head back the way you came for about a third of a mile, and this time turn left at the junction, following the sign to Osmore Pond. You'll pass a trail on the left, and at a four-way junction at 2.7 miles, take a right onto the Osmore Pond Loop Trail. At 3.0 miles you'll come very close to the pond. A short spur trail to the left takes you to the edge.

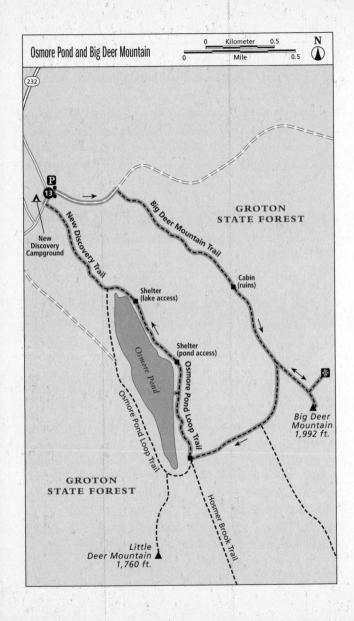

Osmore Pond and Big Deer Mountain

Kilometer
0   0.5
0   0.5
Mile

N

232

P
13

New Discovery Campground

New Discovery Trail

Big Deer Mountain Trail

GROTON STATE FOREST

Shelter (lake access)

Cabin (ruins)

Osmore Pond

Shelter (pond access)

Osmore Pond Loop Trail

Big Deer Mountain 1,992 ft.

Osmore Pond Loop Trail

Hosmer Brook Trail

GROTON STATE FOREST

Little Deer Mountain 1,760 ft.

Following the trail, you will come across two shelters at miles 3.3 and 3.6. These are great places for lunch, and both spots have access to the lake as well as outhouses. After passing by the north end of the lake, the trail climbs gradually for about a half mile, eventually crossing over a dirt road and popping out in the campground. Turn right to get back to where you parked.

Miles and Directions

0.0 Starting from the campground at site 40, head left at the road intersection through the gate to the Big Deer Mountain Trail. (If the gate is open, you can drive to the trailhead, but you'll need to hike back through here at the end of the loop.)

0.3 Turn right onto the Big Deer Mountain Trail.

1.0 Pass by the ruins of an old cabin.

1.4 Go straight at a trail junction, following signs to Big Deer Mountain.

1.75 Reach the summit of Big Deer Mountain. (One viewpoint is straight ahead, and a second is on a short spur just before the end of the trail.)

2.1 After retracing your steps from the summit, turn left at the junction with the trail to Osmore Pond.

2.7 After passing a trail on the left, turn right at four-way junction on the Osmore Pond Loop Trail.

4.1 Cross over a small dirt road.

4.2 Reach the campground and turn right on the road.

4.3 Arrive back at your parking spot.

14 Stowe Pinnacle

The hike up to the Stowe Pinnacle rewards with a mostly treeless summit that provides incredible views of the main spine of the northern Green Mountains to the west, including Mt. Mansfield and Camel's Hump, and the town of Stowe and the Waterbury Reservoir stretching out below.

Distance: 3.6-mile out-and-back
Hiking time: About 2.5 hours
Elevation gain: About 1,500 feet
Difficulty: Moderate
Fees and permits: None
Maps: USGS Quad: Mount Mansfield
Trail contact: Green Mountain Club, (802) 244-7037, www.greenmountainclub.org; Vermont Department of Forests, Parks and Recreation, Main Office Lands Division, (802) 272-4156, www.vtfpr.org
Special considerations: The trail may be closed in late spring to prevent trail damage, so observe posted signs.

Finding the trailhead: On VT 100, 1.5 miles south of the village of Stowe and 8.1 miles north of the intersection with I-89, turn east onto Gold Brook Road. Take the first left, continuing on Gold Brook Road and going through an intersection before hitting a T-junction on Upper Hollow Road 1.8 miles from VT 100. Turn right onto Upper Hollow Road and travel 0.6 mile to the small parking area and trailhead on the left. Trailhead GPS coordinates: N44 26.323' / W72 40.048'

The Hike

The Stowe Pinnacle is actually a sub-peak on the western side of Hogback Mountain. It is a nice straightforward trail with a decent climb and rewards with a fantastic view.

Follow the Stowe Pinnacle Trail straight through a meadow at the top of the short parking area. Soon the trail enters a hardwood forest, first passing by a giant stone rock cairn at 0.3 mile (feel free to add one yourself) and then by a giant teepee made out of sticks and saplings at 0.5 mile.

The trail begins to get steeper with some switchbacks and then briefly levels out at a junction 1 mile into the hike. Here a spur trail leads to Pinnacle Meadow, a conserved area protected by the Stowe Land Trust. (Parking is permitted at Pinnacle Meadow and provides a slightly shorter and less steep access to this junction on the Stowe Pinnacle Trail.)

The trail steepens for a bit here, but shortly leads to a small spur trail to the left with a worthwhile view of Camel's Hump, Mt. Mansfield, and the village of Stowe.

Just when it seems the steep climb will never end, the trail flattens out and contours around the northwest side of the Stowe Pinnacle. After another shorter, steeper climb, the Stowe Pinnacle Trail meets up with the Hogback or Ridge Trail. Following this to the left would lead to the Skyline Trail along the ridge of the Worcester Range.

Go right at this junction, climbing over rocks for another quarter mile until you reach the summit. While the Worcester Range rises above to the immediate east of the summit, a fantastic view north, west, and south makes the climb well worth it. Mt. Mansfield towers over the other side of the valley, while amazing views stretch down the spine of the northern Green Mountains to Camel's Hump and even Mt. Ellen, where the ski trails of Sugarbush are visible. Follow the same route back down to the parking lot.

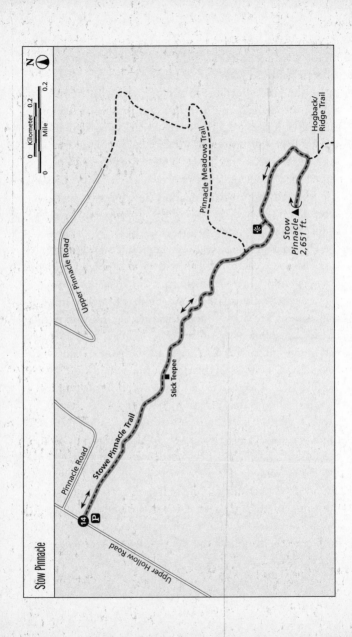

Stow Pinnacle

N

0   Kilometer   0.2
0   Mile   0.2

Pinnacle Road

Stowe Pinnacle Trail

Upper Hollow Road

14 P

Stick Teepee

Upper Pinnacle Road

Pinnacle Meadows Trail

Stow Pinnacle
2,651 ft.

Hogback/
Ridge Trail

Miles and Directions

0.0   The Stowe Pinnacle Trail leaves from the top of the parking area.

0.3   Pass by a giant rock cairn.

0.5   Pass by a large teepee made of sticks and saplings.

1.0   Reach a junction leading to the Pinnacle Meadow parking area. Stay straight and continue on the Stowe Pinnacle Trail.

1.2   Turn left at the sign for a short spur to a beautiful vista. Return to the main trail.

1.5   Go right at the junction with the Hogback/Ridge Trail.

1.8   Reach the summit of Stowe Pinnacle.

3.6   Arrive back at the parking lot via the same route.

15 Camel's Hump via the Burrows Trail

Camel's Hump is one of only five mountains higher than 4,000 feet in Vermont, and is one of the few places with a true alpine environment. The distinctive shape is recognizable from below, and the open summit provides incredible views to New Hampshire, up and down Vermont, and over to New York. The Burrows Trail is one of the easiest ways to climb this tall peak and is very straightforward.

Distance: 4.8-mile out-and-back
Hiking time: About 4 hours
Elevation gain: 2,250 feet
Difficulty: Moderate
Fees and permits: None
Maps: USGS Quad: Huntington
Trail contact: Green Mountain Club, (802) 244-7037, www.greenmountainclub.org; Vermont Department of Forests, Parks and Recreation, Main Office Lands Division, (802) 272-4156, www.vtfpr.org
Special considerations: Weather can be severe up top and it is often windy, so be prepared. Stay on the trail above the tree line, as the alpine vegetation is very fragile and Camel's Hump is one of the most popular hiking destinations in the state.

Finding the trailhead: From I-89 get off on exit 11 and take US 2 east for 2 miles to Bridge Street in the town of Richmond. Turn right on Bridge Street, and in 0.6 mile turn right onto Huntington Road. Follow this road, which turns into Main Road, for 8.9 miles, and turn left on Camel's Hump Road. Follow this road 3.6 miles to a parking lot at the end. Trailhead GPS coordinates: N44 18.294' / W72 54.469'

The Hike

Rising high along the spine of the Green Mountains, Camel's Hump is recognizable by its shape and elevation as one of the most iconic summits in Vermont. This straightforward trail leaves from an elevation close to 2,000 feet, allowing for a fairly quick ascent of the mountain. But don't be fooled; Camel's Hump is a big mountain, and the weather on the summit can be very severe, even on seemingly benign summer days below, so it's best to be prepared with proper attire.

Cross small bridges to the kiosk just up the trail from the parking lot. From here first walk through a rooty and rocky mixed wood, which becomes a beautiful deciduous forest. Keep on going as the forest transitions to birch and spruce, becoming mostly spruce by the time you hit a short rocky section. You will finally burst out of a dense spruce forest into a small clearing, formerly the site of an old lodge, long since destroyed by fire.

This is a good place to get on proper gear for traveling in exposed terrain. Sunglasses and wind protection are necessities on most days. The Long Trail joins here, and this is what you're going to take to the top. Turn right and take the Long Trail heading south. The footing can get a little tough here as you follow the trail over boulders and along short ridges and slabs of rock. Use your hands if you need to.

The trail soon pops above the trees, providing an amazing view north. Not long after, you are on the exposed summit. Stay on the trail and try to step only on rocks, as the vegetation here is extremely fragile. Enjoy panoramic views in all directions, with Mt. Mansfield rising high up not far to the north. You can get a good view of the north-south ridges that make up the Green Mountains from here. Climb just

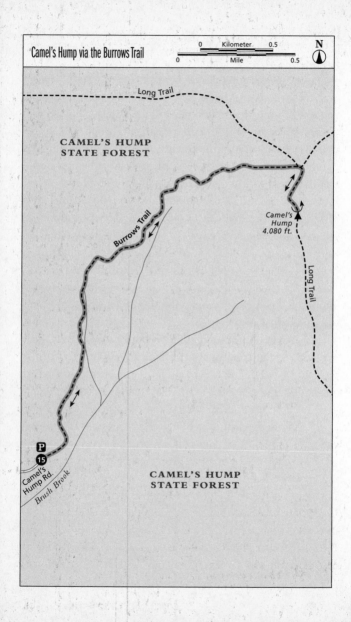

over the other side, following the white Long Trail blazes to the edge of a cliff and a trail over slab on the dramatic south side of the mountain.

Grab a bite to eat sheltered by some rocks and take some photos before heading back down the same trail to the parking lot.

Miles and Directions

0.0 The trail begins at the end of the parking area and leads to a kiosk and register.

2.1 Reach an open area where trails merge. Head right onto the Long Trail, heading south.

2.4 Reach the summit of Camel's Hump.

4.8 Arrive back at the start via the same route.

16 Mt. Mansfield Ridge

Mt. Mansfield is the tallest peak in Vermont. Although this trek costs a little money, the few hours spent traversing the ridge provide unparalleled views without the difficult ascent up the mountain, allowing you to enjoy an afternoon exploring Vermont from a unique alpine environment.

Distance: 2.8-mile out-and-back
Hiking time: About 2 hours
Elevation gain: 500 feet
Difficulty: Moderate (short but rocky)
Fees and permits: There is a fee to drive up the Toll Road.
Maps: USGS Quad: Mount Mansfield
Trail contact: Stowe Mountain Resort, (888) 253-4849, www.stowe.com; Green Mountain Club, (802) 244-7037, www.greenmountainclub.org
Special considerations: The per vehicle Toll Road fee makes it more cost-effective to have several people in your vehicle. The road is open May through Oct from 9 a.m. to 4 p.m. If you want to come down later than 5 p.m., speak with the Toll Road representative where you pay the fee, as they may be able to accommodate your request. The hike traverses the fragile alpine ecosystem, so hikers must stay on the path within the white string and dogs must be leashed and are discouraged from using this trail.

Finding the trailhead: From exit 10 on I-89, follow VT 100 north for 9.5 miles to the town of Stowe. Turn left on VT 108 and follow this for 6 miles to the Toll Road entrance on the left. After paying the fee, climb the dirt road carefully for 4.4 miles, letting descending vehicles have the right of way. Remember to use a low gear on the way down to prevent burning your brakes. Trailhead GPS coordinates: N44 31.688' / W72 48.910'

The Hike

As the highest peak in Vermont, Mt. Mansfield naturally has amazing views, but this hike also provides a beautiful walk through the alpine environment over rocky slabs for a truly unique experience. Although the mountain is far from wild (television and radio towers adorn the top, and Stowe Mountain Resort ski trails cover the east side), the easy access makes it a great trip for hikers of all ages and abilities. As the summit ridge has the profile of a man's face, the prominent features on the mountain are named after facial parts.

From the parking lot, which is situated under the imposing "Nose" of Mt. Mansfield, head up to the visitor center. The sign out front tells you to stay on the trail to prevent damage to the fragile plants. Just beyond the center, head into the woods following the Long Trail north. You'll cross over a private road and pass by the Amherst Trail, shortly reaching the first real viewpoint. From here you can see your path ahead following the obvious ridgeline.

You will follow the white blazes, staying within the string while climbing up and down slabs and rocks and gradually gaining the 500 vertical feet between the parking lot and the "Chin," which is the true summit. You'll pass by a number of trails along the way, including the Cliff Trail at 0.9 mile, which leads down to the gondola. (**Note:** If you have very adventurous souls in your party, the Cliff Trail provides an alternative route back to the parking lot. It is *extremely* steep and rocky, and passes through a slot canyon as well as by a cave that may have snow through August.)

The trail uses plank bridges to cross over fragile marshy areas. Working your way up the rocks, you'll pass by the Sunset Ridge Trail and the Profanity Trail before popping out on

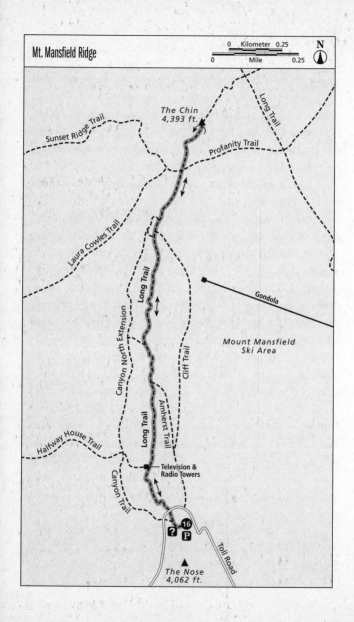

Mt. Mansfield Ridge

0   Kilometer   0.25

0   Mile   0.25

N

Sunset Ridge Trail

The Chin
4,393 ft.

Long Trail

Profanity Trail

Laura Cowles Trail

Long Trail

Canyon North Extension

Gondola

*Mount Mansfield
Ski Area*

Cliff Trail

Long Trail

Amherst Trail

Halfway House Trail

Television &
Radio Towers

Canyon Trail

? 16 P

Toll Road

The Nose
4,062 ft.

the summit. There is often a summit steward from the Green Mountain Club providing helpful information and watching that people stay on the trail.

From here the view is magnificent. Farther north on the ridge is the "Adam's Apple." In the distance you can see Jay Peak and the peaks in Quebec beyond that. Just to the north and east is Smugglers Notch, which is worth a drive through in the summer when the road is open. To the east you can see New Hampshire's White Mountains in the distance, including Mt. Washington, the tallest peak in the state. To the west the equally dominating Adirondacks rise up over Lake Champlain, with New York's highest peak, Mt. Marcy, visible. Following the Green Mountain ridgeline southward, Camel's Hump dominates the view to the south, with other high peaks visible beyond.

Take your time on the summit to enjoy the view, and then return the way you came. You can follow the Long Trail south past the visitor center for another 0.4 mile around the "Nose" to the "Forehead," where a similar, but still impressive, view can be had.

Miles and Directions

0.0 Walk up to the visitor center from the parking lot and head into the woods on the far side, following the Long Trail north.

0.1 Cross a private road and head back into the woods, staying left on the Long Trail at the junction with the Amherst Trail.

0.2 Reach the first obvious viewpoint near the television and radio towers. From here continue following the white blazes on the exposed ridge.

0.5 Stay left at the junction with the Amherst Trail, following the ridge.

0.6 Pass by the junction with the trail to the Canyon North Extension.

0.9 Pass by the junction with the Cliff Trail on the right and two trails in quick succession on the left.

1.2 Pass by the junction with the Sunset Ridge Trail.

1.4 Reach the "Chin" of Mt. Mansfield, the highest point in Vermont.

2.8 Arrive back at the parking lot along the same trail.

17 Indian Brook Reservoir Circumferential Trail

This pleasant stroll around the Indian Brook Reservoir is very easy, and the views along the shore of the lake are beautiful. Make a day of it and picnic and swim, but be sure to check with the Essex Town Office for a parking pass.

Distance: 2.0-mile loop
Hiking time: About 1 hour
Elevation gain: About 100 feet
Difficulty: Easy
Fees and permits: Pass required; purchase during the week at 81 Main Street in Essex, Mon–Fri from 7:30 a.m. to 4 p.m., or call (802) 878-1341 to get information
Maps: USGS Quad: Essex Center

Trail contact: Town of Essex, (802) 878-1341, www.essex.org
Special considerations: This is a great place for dogs, but keep them on leash until you are away from populated areas. *Note:* Parking here requires a pass from the town office; however, recently passes have not been available at times. Check with the town office before beginning the hike.

Finding the trailhead: From the south take exit 12 off I-89 and head north on VT 2A for 3.6 miles to Essex Junction. From the north take exit 15 off I-89 and head 3.7 miles east on VT 15 to Essex Junction. From Essex Junction take VT 15 (Main Street) 2 miles, turn left onto Old Stage Road, and then in 0.4 mile take a left onto Indian Brook Road. The parking at Indian Brook Reservoir is in 1.5 miles. Trailhead GPS coordinates: N44 31.951' / W73 05.731'

The Hike

This nice loop goes around the Indian Brook Reservoir, which can be a great place for a swim, canoe, camp, or just an afternoon picnic. Although the trails aren't well marked in places, you can be sure that if you see the lake, you're doing fine. Only a few short portions of this loop get out of sight of the lake.

To begin the loop, head up the road out of the parking lot. The road ends in a loop, and the trail begins right from there. Follow the east shore of the lake, making sure to bear right at 0.5 mile. Left would take you to the shore and to a campground. Follow an old road for a bit, and just when it seems the road is taking you the wrong way, take a sharp left at a blue arrow at 0.8 mile.

After crossing over Indian Brook on a small bridge, make sure to stay left for the next little while as you head back down the other side of the lake. Continue to keep the lake on your left while bypassing spur trails on the right, including the McGee Trail at 1.3 miles, all the way to the end of the Circumferential Trail, which links up with the parking lot at a gravel trail below the dam at the southern terminus of the reservoir.

Miles and Directions

0.0 Begin at the parking lot.

0.1 Walk up from the parking lot to the loop at the end of the road, where the trail begins.

0.5 Turn right at the intersection where a spur trail leads left to campground.

0.8 Turn left at an intersection, following the blue arrow.

0.9 At the intersection with the North Bay Trail, head right, continuing to follow the Circumferential Trail.

1.3 Go straight/left at the intersection with the McGee Trail.

1.7 Stay left at an intersection with a spur trail.

1.9 Follow the gravel path below the dam back to the parking lot.

2.0 Arrive back at the parking lot.

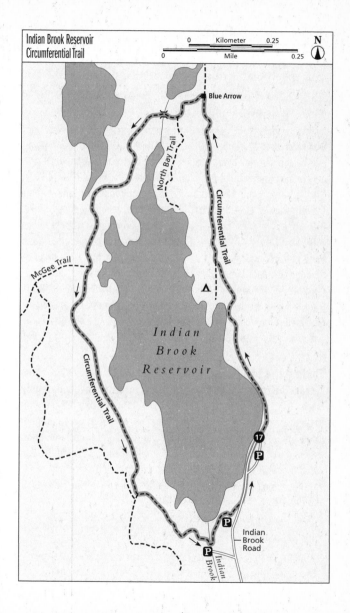

Indian Brook Reservoir
Circumferential Trail

Kilometer

Mile

N

Blue Arrow

North Bay Trail

McGee Trail

Circumferential Trail

Circumferential Trail

Indian
Brook
Reservoir

17

Indian
Brook Road

Indian Brook

18 Rock Point

This collection of paths on private land owned by the Episcopal Diocese provides incredible views of Lake Champlain from a few spots along a cliff.

Distance: About 2.2-mile out-and-back plus small loop (varies depending on what trails you take)
Hiking time: About 1.5 hours
Elevation gain: Less than 100 feet (varies)
Difficulty: Easy
Fees and permits: Pass required; available from Episcopal Diocese of Vermont, Mon–Fri 9 a.m.–4 p.m. at the diocese office; weekend visitors must call ahead at (800) 286-3437

Maps: USGS Quad: Burlington
Trail contact: Episcopal Diocese of Vermont, (802) 863-3431
Special considerations: In addition to obtaining a pass to hike, observe all signs, respect the private property, carry out all trash, stay on trails, and keep dogs leashed. No bicycles allowed; respect summer campers. Donations are greatly appreciated.

Finding the trailhead: From I-89 head west on VT 2/Main Street through the city of Burlington, and in 1.9 miles turn right on Battery Street, which becomes Park Street. Travel 0.8 mile, turn left on Manhattan Drive, and in 0.3 mile go right onto North Avenue. Head north for 0.7 mile; then take a left on Institute Road, pass a school, and turn right onto Rock Point Road in 0.2 mile, heading toward the Episcopal Diocese. The parking lot is on the right in a quarter mile, and the office is just across the road from the parking lot. Trailhead GPS coordinates: N44 29.802'/W73 14.415'

The Hike

The unique property, which is situated on a rocky peninsula that reaches out into Lake Champlain, provides incredible cliff-top views of the lake and of the Adirondack Mountains to the west. As this is private property and requires permission to hike, be sure to stay on the signed paths and do not veer off into the woods following unofficial trails.

After receiving the necessary permits and information, follow the road to the trailhead, first taking a left at a fork (signed) and then taking the road to the actual trailhead in a half mile. A guided numbered sign here points out spots of interest. Head straight/left as you pass through an open field called the parade grounds. Continue straight ahead, and at the first junction a short spur trail will lead down to the shore past the interesting thrust fault geologic feature.

Return to this junction, and continue straight along the edge of the peninsula past a number of viewpoints to Lone Rock Point, the obvious large rocky promontory near the end of the peninsula. Although there are a number of trails in various states of use, head back along the same trail to the previous junction. From here head left up a short, steeper section to another good view. Then, following signs, turn right on the trail to the outdoor chapel. This will lead back to the original junction. Follow your steps back to the parking lot.

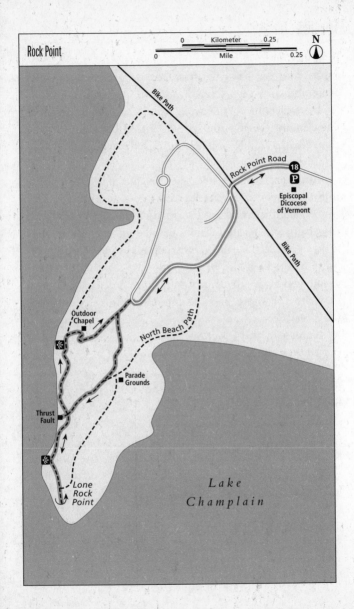

Rock Point

0   Kilometer   0.25

0   Mile   0.25

N

Bike Path

Rock Point Road

18

P

Episcopal
Dicocese
of Vermont

Bike Path

Outdoor
Chapel

North Beach Path

Parade
Grounds

Thrust
Fault

Lone
Rock
Point

*Lake
Champlain*

Miles and Directions

0.0 Continue along the road on which you arrived.

0.1 Cross over a bridge and bear left at the fork in the road.

0.5 Pass by the bishop's house and a few other buildings to reach the signed trailhead.

0.6 Reach the junction of trails. Bear straight/left.

0.7 Reach a trail junction. A short spur straight ahead leads to the thrust fault and canoe landing. From the junction follow the trail to the left.

1.0 After passing by a few viewpoints, you'll reach Lone Rock Point. Turn around and follow the trail back to the junction.

1.3 At the junction head left up an incline.

1.4 After a viewpoint turn right near a fence to follow a trail to the outdoor chapel.

1.5 Reach the outdoor chapel. Follow the trail back to the first major junction.

1.6 Reach the original junction and head back to the parking lot via the same route.

2.2 Arrive back at the parking lot.

19 Devil's Gulch and Ritterbush Pond

This nice loop hike will take you to a few pleasant outlooks, the edge of a beautiful pond, and the amazing Devil's Gulch, which involves a fun rocky scramble through a deep gorge.

Distance: 5.9-mile loop
Hiking time: About 3 to 4 hours
Elevation gain: About 900 feet
Difficulty: Moderate to difficult
Fees and permits: None
Maps: USGS Quad: Eden

Trail contact: Green Mountain Club, (802) 244-7037, www.greenmountainclub.org
Special considerations: Although Devil's Gulch itself is less than a quarter mile long, it is not recommended for most dogs.

Finding the trailhead: From I-89, get off on exit 10, heading north on VT 100. Follow VT 100 for 29.5 miles to the town of Eden, and then take a left onto VT 118. The parking lot for the trailhead is located 4.7 miles ahead on the right. It is a sharp turnoff to the right after you go most of the way around a big left-hand curve. The parking area is a bit hidden, so look carefully for a sign for the Long Trail. If you reach Belvidere Pond, which comes right up to the road, you've gone too far. Trailhead GPS coordinates: N44 45.838' / W72 35.250'

The Hike

This loop, although longer than most hikes in this book, is a fairly easy way to get good views and has a fun scramble through a cool gorge on the Long Trail. Due to the location of this hike, it is a great place to visit on a busy weekend, as you will likely encounter very few other hikers.

Start from the sign in the parking lot and follow the Long Trail south along a short trail in the woods, cross VT 118, follow the road for about 25 yards to the left, and head right into the woods back on the trail. After gradually rising along a pleasant woods trail, you will begin to descend, sometimes down nice stone steps, to a shaded outlook onto Ritterbush Pond at 1.4 miles.

The trail descends while paralleling the shore until reaching the Babcock Trail junction. A short out-and-back down the spur trail on the left takes you to a dirt road and, after a quick jaunt left, to the edge of Ritterbush Pond, where you can personally check out some nice beaver cutting.

After returning to the Long Trail, turn left, continuing the way you were going. In less than a half mile, you will make a jog to the right up a short ladder and reach the sign for Devil's Gulch. Follow the trail ahead, and soon you'll see the main feature of the gorge, two giant rocks leaning against each other, creating a tunnel. Walls rise up on both sides, and lush foliage blankets the moist floor during summer. Enjoy this cool respite.

Instead of heading back, it is worth the extra effort to head to Devil's Perch viewpoint. Continue through the gulch on the Long Trail as it heads up to the left following a small stream. You'll reach the junction for Spruce Ledge Camp at 2.9 miles. Follow this to the camp and a nice bench just beyond with incredible views. Below is Ritterbush Pond, and ahead you'll see Belvidere Mountain with the fire tower on top. You'll also see a large white mound on the side of the mountain, which is a huge asbestos tailings pile from a mining operation.

Retrace your steps all the way back to the Babcock Trail junction. This time turn left (north) on the Babcock Trail. It

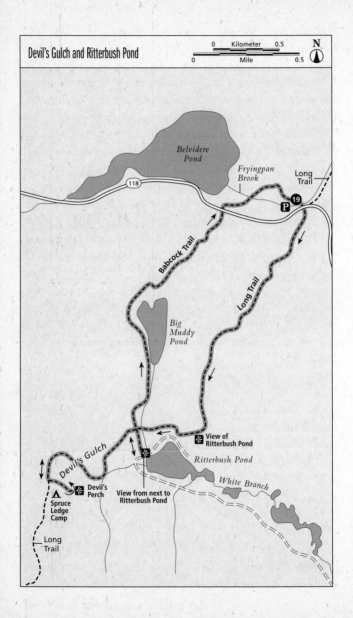

Devil's Gulch and Ritterbush Pond

Kilometer 0   0.5
Mile   0   0.5

N

Belvidere Pond

Fryingpan Brook

Long Trail

118

P 19

Babcock Trail

Long Trail

Big Muddy Pond

View of Ritterbush Pond

Ritterbush Pond

Devil's Gulch

View from next to Ritterbush Pond

White Branch

Devil's Perch

Spruce Ledge Camp

Long Trail

will head up over a rise and then pass by the beautiful Big Muddy Pond. Continue until you reach VT 118. Cross the road here, and follow the blue-blazed trail onto a dirt road. You will follow this for about a quarter mile, keeping an eye out on the right for where the trail heads back into the woods and a short while later reaches the parking lot.

Miles and Directions

0.0   From the sign at the end of the parking lot, head up a short slope, following the Long Trail south.

0.1   Cross over VT 118 and follow the road 25 yards to the left until you reach the slightly hidden entrance to the Long Trail on the right.

1.4   Reach a small view of Ritterbush Pond.

1.7   Turn left at the junction with the Babcock Trail.

1.85   Reach the edge of Ritterbush Pond.

2.0   Return to the junction of Babcock Trail. Turn left, continuing to follow the Long Trail south.

2.5   After turning slightly right and climbing a short ladder, you will reach the sign for Devil's Gulch.

2.7   Leave Devil's Gulch, continuing to follow the Long Trail gradually up and to the left.

2.9   Turn left at the junction for the Spruce Ledge Camp.

3.0   Reach Devil's Perch viewpoint just past the camp. Return via the same route.

4.0   At the junction with the Babcock Trail, turn left to follow the Babcock Trail north.

5.5   Reach the trail register and VT 118. Follow the trail across the road, shortly meeting up with a dirt road.

5.7   Turn right off the dirt road and follow the trail.

5.9   Arrive back at the parking area.

20 Wheeler Mountain

This short but challenging loop hike offers some fun steep rock scrambling, a walk along a cliff, and amazing views of Lake Willoughby and some of the high peaks of Vermont.

Distance: 2.4-mile out-and-back with loop
Hiking time: About 2 hours
Elevation gain: 700 feet
Difficulty: Moderate (the Red Trail is steeper than the White Trail)
Fees and permits: None
Maps: USGS Quad: Lyndonville
Trail contact: Westmore Trail Association, Town Clerk Office, Hilton Hill Rd., Westmore, 05822, (802) 525-3007, www.westmore oline.org/main/; Vermont Department of Forests, Parks and Recreation, Main Office Lands Division, (802) 272-4156, www.vtfpr.org
Special considerations: This hike has a dirt road access, so avoid in the muddy season. There are sections of open slab, so this hike is not ideal for those afraid of heights, and it is very slippery when wet, so avoid if rain is in the forecast.

Finding the trailhead: From I-91 take US 5 north. You will travel through Lyndonville, and in 9.5 miles at the junction of VT 5A in West Burke, continue left on US 5 north and travel another 8.3 miles. Turn right on Wheeler Mountain Road. Follow this dirt road for 1.9 miles until you reach a small parking lot on the left. If the lot is full, please don't block the road with your car. Trailhead GPS coordinates: N44 43.668'/W72 05.808'

The Hike

Follow the road back down for about a minute, and you'll see the trailhead on the right. The trail dips and soon crosses a stream. Stay right here, and soon you'll reach a junction of the White and Red Trails. The White Trail continues along a big field, while the Red Trail heads into the woods. Follow the Red Trail to the right. (For those less inclined to scrambling up steep rocks, going up and down the White Trail may be a better option.)

After climbing for another 0.2 mile, you'll get a nice vista to the south. Follow along the base of the cliff for a short while; then follow the red blazes painted on the rock straight up the steep slab. Follow the three-point rule by carefully placing each foot, and make sure you have three points of contact, either two feet and one hand or vice versa. The edge of the trail may have some easier holds as well. It may seem intimidating, but any reasonably fit child or adult should have no problem carefully climbing the route.

The Red Trail pops out into a more open area and soon rejoins the White Trail at 0.5 mile. Just above this junction is a great little rocky knoll. Wheeler Pond is visible just to the south, and on the knoll there are incredible views west to Jay Peak and the northern Green Mountains.

Follow the trail just below this knoll back into the woods for a bit as it quickly pops out on a fun little rock ridge at the top of the Wheeler Mountain cliffs. Follow this ridge for a short way, and then follow the trail back into the woods along a short rooty section.

The trail emerges from the woods at Eagle Point, where there is a register and outlook with amazing views. To the east lies Lake Willoughby, Vermont's deepest lake, flanked by the steep slopes of Mt. Hor and Mt. Pisgah. On a clear day you can see a number of wind turbines along a ridge to the south.

Follow the trail back the way you came, but take a right at the junction of the White and Red Trails, following the

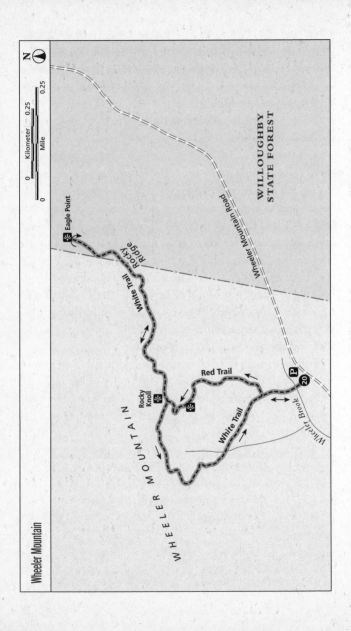

Wheeler Mountain

WILLOUGHBY
STATE FOREST

Eagle Point

Rocky Ridge

White Trail

Rocky Knoll

Red Trail

White Trail

Wheeler Mountain Road

WHEELER MOUNTAIN

Wheeler Brook

P
20

N

0   Kilometer   0.25

0   Mile   0.25

white trail blazes back down through the woods. Although there are no steep rocky slabs, this trail is steep and rooty, so take your time. Cross over a small stream, then follow along the edge of a big field, and finally cross back over Wheeler Brook to the trailhead.

Miles and Directions

0.0 Leave from the trailhead, which is about 100 feet south of the parking area on Wheeler Mountain Road.

0.1 At the first junction of the Red and White Trails, turn right onto the Red Trail.

0.3 Skirt along the base of a rocky ledge to a nice view to the south.

0.5 Stay straight/right at the upper junction with the White Trail. Just above the junction is a nice rocky knoll for views to the south. Keep right and go into the woods.

0.8 Follow open ledge on the edge of the cliff; then briefly head back into the woods.

1.1 Reach Eagle Point, your destination. Turn around and retrace route.

1.7 At the junction of the White and Red Trails, stay right (west) on the White Trail.

2.4 Arrive back at the trailhead.

About the Author

Eli Burakian is a professional photographer. He has worked on numerous books with Globe Pequot and FalconGuides. He also wrote and photographed *Moosilauke: A Portrait of a Mountain*. He is an avid skier and hiker and spends any time he can playing in the outdoors. He currently works for Dartmouth College as the college photographer, and he lives with his wife, son, and two dogs in Windsor, Vermont. Visit him at BurakianPhotography.com.